M

一種開着乳白色花朵的樹上的嫩葉時，發現這種綠葉真奇怪，一到肚子裡，就從上到下，到處流動洗滌，好似把腸胃洗滌得乾乾淨淨。他就推語這種綠葉對人體有醫療效用，看要經過一段漫長的歲月。當原始人類發現茶葉對人體的利用，茶和其他植物一樣，從發現到利用，看要經過一段漫長的歲月。到了春秋戰國時代，已經提到用茶葉作藥飲，但沒有專門作為飲料的記錄。

據古籍記載，茶葉最初只作藥用，茶就開始被注意和重視起來。同時，傳播到當時的經濟、政治、文化中心陝西、河南等地傳播，開始向當時的經濟、文化的交流，造成了人口的大遷徙。特別是蜀統一中國以後，促進了經濟和文化的交流，造成了人口的大遷徙。

戰國後期及西漢初年，曾發生過幾次大規模的戰爭。

有人認為「秦人取蜀」，即產茶和飲茶始於秦漢時。有的人認為「秦人取蜀（四川），而後始有茗飲之事」，即產茶和飲茶始於秦漢時。到三國時，吳末帝皓因大臣韋曜酒量太小，曾在宴會上密賜韋曜以茶代酒，於是有人認為中國現存最早和最有價值的茶葉作為飲料了。

有許多文獻的記錄。到了春秋時代，已經提到用茶葉作藥飲，但沒有作為日常的飲料記錄。有許多文獻的記錄。有定論。有許多文獻記載。

作者說衆說紛紜，對茶葉有一段關於漢代飲茶的記載：漢成帝崩，「后（即帝后）寢驚啼甚久，侍帝呼問，方覺，乃言因夢中見帝，帝自云中賜吾坐，帝命進茶。左右奏帝，后向日侍帝不謹，不合啜此茶。」反映在西漢時期，茶已成為皇室中的一種飲料了。又據史料記載，漢王曾在江蘇宜奧茗嶺「課童藝茶」。浙江臨海蓋竹山有仙翁茗嶺，漢朝名士葛玄曾植茗於此。浙江餘姚人虞洪，往年回紇入山採茗，遇仙人丹丘子，獲得大茗，等等。說明當時在江蘇、浙江一帶，已有茶樹栽植，並有過去長期積累下來的茶樹栽培和製茶經驗。

茶葉作為珍貴的貢品，由此可以推想到西漢以前，即公元前二十一世紀至公元前十一世紀，應可知唐時飲茶之風，已由南方傳到黃河北岸，茶的起源距今當有三、四千年的歷史了。王褒的《僮約》是唐朝大曆名馬市茶而歸。可知唐時飲茶之風，已由南方傳到黃河北岸，茶的葡萄牙凱薩琳公主嫁給英王查理二世時，成了中國第一個飲茶的國家。

到了明萬曆四十六年（公元一六一八年），我國已有茶葉作為珍貴的禮品經陸路運給蘇聯。明隆慶元年（公元一五六七年），有兩位俄國人首次將茶葉從陸路運回國內，而茶葉傳入國人日首次將中國的消息傳回國內。

福茗堂茶莊

狀元梅花水片

六安包種

福茗堂茶莊

本號在太子行 開張檢提細嫩 茶葉加芽揉造 發行 香港中環遮打道太子行 商場二百十一室

金圓貢品烏龍

鐵觀音

狀元梅花水片

福茗堂 本號在太子行 開張檢提細嫩 茶葉加芽揉造 發行 香港中環遮打道太子行 商場二百十一室

本號在太子行 開張檢提細嫩 茶葉加芽揉造 發行 香港中環遮打道太子行 商場二百十一室

THE BOOK OF TEA

PREFACE
BY ANTHONY BURGESS

ARTISTIC DIRECTION
MARC WALTER

TRANSLATED
BY DEKE DUSINBERRE

Flammarion

CONTENTS

■

◆ PREFACE ◆

by Anthony Burgess

Samuel Pepys, the diarist of the reign of Charles II, who came to the British throne in 1660, writes of having drunk "tee (a China drinke) of which I had never drank before." He does not say whether he liked it or not. There was at first some dissension as to its preparation. It could be either too strong or too weak. Should it be sweetened or not? In the eighteenth century the greatest tea drinker of all time established the way the British were to drink it. This was Dr. Samuel Johnson, the lexicographer who created his huge English Dictionary single-handed, no doubt under the stimulation of tea. His teapot held two litres. He took it strong, the bite of the tannin being allayed with a little milk, adding sugar in little lumps. At the house of a distinguished lady, he kept passing his cup for more and more, until he had ingested thirty-two cups. The lady said: "Dr. Johnson, you drink too much tea." Johnson said "Madam, you are insolent." Clearly, the very British institution of the tea party, or what the French call *le five o'clock*, had been established by this time. It still goes on. Tea has become not merely the name of a beverage but the name of a meal. Sandwiches and cakes accompany the cheerful cups. In the north of England, where the meal is called "high tea," there are lamb chops and fried potatoes as well. The tea is, so to speak, swamped by the circumambient food. But it is still there, hot, strong and copious.

The first British tea drinkers got their leaf from China. But the stronger and less delicate varieties from India and Ceylon have tended to dominate the market (whose centre is Mincing Lane, in the heart of that part of London known as the

Wry humor and the love of tea are both quintessentially English characteristics. On average, the English drink six cups per day per person, rivaling the Chinese as the world's heaviest consumers of tea. *Opposite:* A chambermaid in Cambridge in 1939, during the ritual tea break that punctuated the working day.

City). China tea is for exquisite people like Oscar Wilde; his compatriots, still living in Ireland, demand the brutal overstewed Indian variety. The Irish taste in tea is also the taste of the British working class. Most tea-addicts of humble origins, such as myself, will opt for Twining's Irish Breakfast Tea—the leaf or the sachet—with Twining's Darjeeling as a close competitor. The drawing rooms of the ruling class prefer the perfume of Earl Gray or Lapsang. The lower orders, given tea in a pot with thimble-sized cups in a Chinese restaurant, accept the exotic bestowal but do not take it seriously. After the meal, they go home and brew some real, meaning Indian or Ceylon, tea. The Russian way, passed on to the immigrant Jews of Britain, is unacceptable to the British gentile on two counts—there is no milk, and the beverage is served in a glass. But it is strong (Russian Caravan tea has none of the fragile allure of the Chinese variety) and it is sweetened with a spoonful of jam. But a *stakan chai*—a glass of tea—is a frightening anomaly. Tea is not tea to the British unless it is poured into a cup.

A cup, yes, but there is a class division centred on what precisely is meant by a cup. The upper class have the most exquisite china, but the tea poured into it is a mere mouthful. A mug—a much larger cup with no saucer—is the lower-class receptacle. The class division was made almost blatantly clear in World War II, when the commissioned officers took their tea in upper-class china in the officers' mess, while the rest of the army was issued with a mug that held half a litre of tea brewed coarsely in a bucket (flavoured with cigarette ash or even rhinoid mucus). The Asterix cartoon about the tea-maddened Britons was a kind of retrospective prophecy: Britain could not have fought either of the two major wars of our century without tea.

The really important beverage division concerns itself with tea and coffee. Tea versus coffee? In the eighteenth century, London had its coffee houses, where hot chocolate was also served. There were no tea houses: these were an oriental affectation. Tea was for home consumption. Coffee is always difficult to brew, and few British homes offer a good cup of it.

"It is proper both for Winter and Summer, preserving in perfect health until extreme old age, it maketh the body active and lusty . . . it removeth lassitude and cleanseth acrid humours. . . ." Thus Thomas Garraway praised the virtues of tea in the mid-seventeenth century. Garraway was the first to import the magic potion from China and sell it in England. *Above:* In the French comic book series *Asterix*, the heroic Gaul of the title concocts this "barbarous" potion for a Breton warrior, who comments that the recipe seems easy enough. *Opposite:* A portable tea trolley at Wimbledon on 21 June 1937 enables tennis fans who have lined up in front of ticket windows since dawn to rid themselves of "lassitude."

Instant coffee is served with a certain gloom: no one really likes it, but the making of the real thing is beyond the powers of British home technology. Coffee-making is for professionals, and the professionals made it in the eighteenth-century coffee houses. Some of these were not only famous for their brew: they were the centres of political and literary argument, like Wills's. Lloyd's coffee house, which purveyed the latest shipping news as one of its amenities, became the greatest insurance centre in the world. Tea has never been associated with public life. It is too domestic. It is sometimes, as for instance by Ian Fleming's creation James Bond, considered a drink for women. Coffee, like the brandy that accompanies it, is for men. The working class begs to differ.

That there is a kind of enmity between tea and coffee is supposed to be illustrated by the revolt of the American colonies from British rule. The New England Americans drank tea like their cousins in the homeland, but they resented the heavy tax imposed on it by the government in London. Hence the Boston Tea Party, in which patriotic Americans, dressed as Mohawk Indians, hurled whole tons of the imported leaf into Boston harbour. This led to the War of Independence and the tradition of American coffee-drinking in imitation of the French. The Americans, just like the French, do not know how to make tea. One of Graham Greene's characters knows that he is in Paris when he sees a man at an open-air café dipping a teabag into tepid water, holding it by its stringy tail like a mouse. The Americans have forgotten the art they brought over from Britain: they too are great teabag-dippers.

In American hotels, from Vermont to Florida, I have pleaded with waiters and waitresses for strong tea. I always end up with warm water and a sachet of Earl Gray. At a Holiday Inn I gave detailed instructions. Take one of those coffee jugs. Place in it six bags of Lipton's or Twining's Indian or Ceylon. Pour on boiling water. Bring it to me. This was, in a manner, done for me in Minneapolis. The only trouble was that the six bags had been stewed in warm coffee. A coffee jug was for coffee; ergo, coffee had to be in it. I tend now to travel through the United States with my own half-litre mug and electric kettle. This is considered very British.

Before I go further, it would be in order for me to state here how precisely tea ought to be prepared. First, you must have a capacious teapot. Then you must have a kettle. Boil your water and at the

In England, establishments that serve tea have always been considered ideal meeting places for people from all walks of life. The original coffee houses (Thomas Twining opened one that also served tea as early as 1706) evolved into tea gardens and eventually into tea rooms. Such places are increasingly rare, unfortunately, and in present-day London, afternoon tea is served mainly in the grand hotels. *Opposite:* Two enlisted soldiers on leave enjoy afternoon tea at a Lyons Corner House on Coventry Street in 1926.

same time heat your teapot. It is unwise to heat it by swilling warm water around in it: it will be difficult to swill all of this out, and thus the inside of the teapot will be wet. It must be perfectly dry. Place the teapot in an inch or so of very hot water; when its external bottom is hot enough to make the hand uncomfortable, its internal bottom is hot enough for tea. Place into the warmed pot, according to the tradition, one teaspoonful for each drinker and an extra teaspoonful as a gift for the pot. You may, of course, increase these doses according to taste or, more accurately, to habituation. I substitute a dessert spoon for a teaspoon. Pour on boiling water from the kettle. Stir the infusion gently. Place the lid on the pot and leave it for five minutes. Then pour into cup or mug.

If you take milk with your tea—no more than a minute amount to soften the impact of the tannin content—you must decide which faction to belong to—the one that puts the milk into the cup before pouring the tea, or the school that drips milk in while the tea lies black and

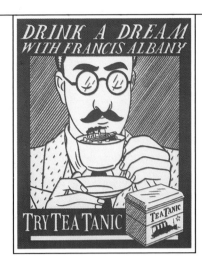

DRINK A DREAM
WITH FRANCIS ALBANY

TRY TEA TANIC

TEA TANIC

steaming. I do not think it makes very much difference: it is one of these very British controversies which keep off the *tedium vitae*. You may then add sugar, but this is frowned upon by many tea-drinking experts. The late George Orwell was one of these. He published an essay, rather less well-known than his *Nineteen Eighty-Four* (one of the horrors of which seems to be a total absence of tea, though not gin), whose title is "A Nice Cup of Tea." In it he says that the addition of sugar kills the taste of the tea. He also says that the older one grows the stronger one prefers one's tea. One of the few good qualities he found in Britain's wartime Ministry of Food was its willingness to grant a larger ration of tea to citizens over 65 (60 if they were women) than to the younger and unseasoned.

Tea, though so much a feature of the British scene, is a highly exotic substance. Nazi U-boats sank a great many of the merchant vessels bringing food to British shores, especially in the Atlantic, but exiguous imports of tea came in from India

In Great Britain, as in many other places, taking tea is often a subtle and refined occasion that requires a small measure of artistry. To savor tea time fully, one must know how to take the time to relax, how to leave daily cares behind and appreciate the simple pleasures of the moment. It is thus associated with luxury, whatever the circumstances, and is often conducive to wit and good humor, particularly among the English. *Above:* A silkscreen by Floc'h and Rivière, the *Tea Tanic*, produced in conjunction with their comic book, *A la Recherche de Sir Malcolm. Opposite:* On the deck of a transatlantic liner in the 1920s.

and Ceylon: the Japanese naval force was busy in the Pacific but not so much in the Indian Ocean, and the British Navy kept the tea-lines open in the Red Sea and the Mediterranean. Without tea Britain could not have fought the war. A novel by Len Deighton called *SS-GB* presents an imaginary England under the heel of the Germans from 1940 on (an analogue of the French situation). There is tea available for the enslaved British, but it is in a powdered form and its flavour is of *ersatz* lemon. That is the way the Nazi occupying troops prefer it. Deighton's characters suffer but do not revolt. Here the book is less than plausible. Without real tea the enslaved British would have risked the perils of insurrection. I do not exaggerate. We cannot do without it.

It is, if you wish, a drug, though the drop of milk relates it to our mother's wholesome breasts. Dr. Johnson's biographer, James Boswell, feared that the Grand Cham's perpetual consumption of strong tea might injure his nerves. But, though the tannin may, in some feeble instances, harm the digestive system, it will do so far less than will the French wine so many of us are abandoning. For wine is increasingly charged with tannin. There is still a British superstition that to drink strong tea with a grilled steak, or the Sunday slices of roast beef, literally tans the meat and turns it to leather. This is a small price to pay for the enlivening effect of a morning, mid-morning, lunchtime, afternoon, evening, late evening, and midnight pot of tea. I say pot advisedly, and I imply tea in the leaf, not the sachet. For there are rumours that the paper of the teabag is not altogether healthy; there is an obscure reaction between the chemical substances in the leaf and its dioxin-soaked container which brings on some disease or other. But the teabag, however convenient, was always, anyway, a travesty of the loaded spoon and its aromatic heap of the real thing.

Teabags tend to be preferred these days because the disposal of the infused, spent, soggy tea leaves in the cold pot is difficult. You cannot swill them down the kitchen sink without risking the clogging of the drains. To pour them into the toilet and flush them down lends an excremental flavour to what has been a civilised potation. Hens like them mixed with old bread, but few people keep hens. You can spread them lightly on the floor and sweep them away along with the dust they attract. You can keep them in the teapot and bring them back to life with boiling water, but

In 1942, Churchill claimed that tea was more important to his soldiers than ammunition. All the English agreed that their morale would not have withstood the bombing, nor would their army have defeated the Afrika Korps, if they had been deprived of their national beverage. Tea was the ultimate British weapon during World War II, for it was not only a comfort but also a rare pleasure, and therefore a powerful symbol of freedom. *Opposite:* An example of the family shelters that civil defense organizations designed and promoted among the civilian population.

their vitality has vanished and you are drinking a ghost. They are a nuisance when their usefulness is past, just like people. But to prefer teabags to real tea is to exalt the shadow over the substance.

The substance remains so magical that it is strange that it has been so little celebrated in the arts. It was a Frenchman, Maurice Ravel, who celebrated *le five o'clock* in a jazzy dance in *L'Enfant et les sortilèges*, but no Englishman has produced a musical work on tea analogous to Bach's *Coffee Cantata*. A member of parliament, A. P. Herbert, wrote a vapid song with the refrain "A Nice Cup of Tea" (a cup of tea is always "nice" in England, just as a beefsteak is always *una bella bistecca* in Italy). The poet William Cowper praised "the cups that cheer but not inebriate." But there the literature of tea comes to an end. I doubt if there is an English book devoted to tea. Here, however, is a French one. Perhaps tea is so woven into the stomach linings of the British that they cannot view it in either a scholarly or an aesthetic manner. It is a fact of British life, like breathing.

A nice cup of tea taken to delightful excess. *Above:* "The largest teapot in the world," displayed at the 1938 Empire Exhibition, boasted a two-gallon capacity. *Opposite:* On a sweltering summer day in 1947, typists from the City (London's business district) take a tea break at the Endell Street pool.

· TEA ·

GARDENS

Alain Stella

To find out what all of the world's finest tea gardens—from the Far East to West Africa—have in common, stroll through one at nightfall. At this hour, the gardens resemble one another. They are brushed by the same thick clouds and cool mountain air, and cleansed by the same rain. They all proffer a concert of rainfall on leaves, of swollen torrents and cascades, and they all exude the same odors of warm, moist earth. For wherever it is cultivated, tea will impart its highly sought, subtle fragrances only if grown in a wet and temperate climate—long sunny days followed by rainy nights and pure mountain breezes.

It is only at daybreak, when the first birds break into song and clouds scatter beyond the horizon or nestle low in the valleys, when the sun's rays transform the mist into a glittery dew on the leaves, that the infinite variety of tea gardens slowly becomes apparent. From this standpoint, every estate looks different, from Japan to Cameroon. Suddenly nothing is the same, from the color of the soil, to the shape of the hills, to the surrounding greenery, to the women weaving their way toward the gardens at this early hour.

Dawn breaks over the tea gardens of Asia. *Above:* A plantation in Ceylon, the "Isle of Tea." *Opposite:* Mount Kangchenjunga (28,208 feet), legendary abode of the god Shiva, rises above the Darjeeling district in northeastern India. *Page 20:* Nurturing a new shoot at a garden in Nilgiri, southwestern India. All tea plants belong to the same species—*Camellia sinensis*—although three main varieties exist (China, Assam, and Indochina). Young plants are grown in the shade of a nursery for at least a year before being transplanted into the garden.

DARJEELING

In the northeast Indian region of Darjeeling, between Sikkim, Nepal, and Bhutan, women climb the mountain paths every day at dawn. They make their way toward one of the sixty-one gardens that produce the highly prized "champagne" of black teas on grand estates perched at altitudes of over five thousand feet. The women, strapping Himalaya-dwellers with prominent cheekbones and narrow eyes, advance in single file. Their clothes are poor, but some women wear a silver stud in one nostril. Far behind them, set against the rose-hued sky, loom the eternally mysterious snows of Kangchenjunga, a mountain over twenty-six thousand feet high, said to be the abode of the god Shiva. The women continue to climb above the charming villas and hotels of Darjeeling (where Calcutta's upper middle classes come to escape the noxious monsoon season). They encounter schoolgirls in red dresses and farmers heading for the small village markets. Then, after several winding turns between rock faces on which climbers train, the women finally arrive at the garden.

The garden might be named Castleton, Jungpana, Tukvar, or Badamtam. In Darjeeling, what is called a "garden" is in fact a large plantation sometimes stretching over a thousand acres. But it is still a "garden" because the tea grown here, harvested according to traditional methods, bears its name. Darjeeling's sixty-one gardens produce fifteen thousand tons of tea per year. Its incomparable quality is the result of climate, altitude, and British expertise, plus a disdain for quantity. The wide range of Darjeeling teas is obtained through skillful blending (which varies

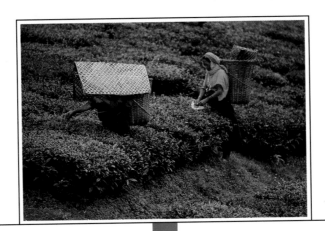

A traditional harvest in the Himalayan foothills of Darjeeling, where some of the finest tea in the world—known as the "champagne" of teas—matures at an altitude of 6,500 feet. *Above:* Pluckers working in the rain. Moisture is a key factor in tea cultivation, for the plant requires regular, steady rainfall. *Opposite:* One of the sixty-one Darjeeling gardens at plucking time. The steep mountain slopes, which inhibit mechanization and impose traditional harvesting methods, help to ensure outstanding quality.

according to the altitude of the estate) of the large-leaved plants from Assam with the smaller but robust leaves of Chinese plants. These two main varieties of the single species of tea plant—*Camellia sinensis*—are sometimes crossbred into hybrids. A wild tea plant from China grows six to nine feet high and lives for over one hundred years. An Assam plant can grow to be sixty feet high if unpruned, but does not live beyond fifty years.

Chinese plants, more resistant to cold, are commonly found on plantations in northern Darjeeling, often at altitudes of over six thousand feet. To the south, where plantations are generally located at one thousand feet, Assam plants are more suited to the abundant rainfall.

The diversity of Darjeeling tea is further accentuated by differences in wind and rainfall that depend on the altitude and exposure of the slopes under cultivation. Yet it is seasonal changes that produce the most marked differences. Although tea-lovers cannot always tell a Makaibari from a Puttabong, they can immediately distinguish between a Selimbong tea harvested in spring ("first flush," from late February to mid-April) and the same tea harvested in early summer ("second flush," in May and June), or autumn ("autumnal," in October and November).

The women arrive at the garden just as the sun appears above the snowy peaks. Everywhere in the world, fine tea requires an average of five hours of sun per day. The plantation forms an immense green carpet covering the slopes of the Himalayan foothills. It hugs the dramatic curves, slinking down valleys to riverbeds, climbing to the summit of peaks. It is not unusual for plants to be terraced on 45-degree inclines where

Once picked, tea is immediately dispatched to the factory where it is processed. Transportation time must be kept to a minimum to retain the freshness of the tea, so factories are located on the plantations themselves. Every large garden possesses its own factory. *Above:* The factory at Makaibari, one of Darjeeling's most famous gardens. *Opposite:* A preliminary stage in processing tea in Darjeeling involves sorting freshly plucked leaves by hand to obtain the desired quality.

no machine could ever venture. This mountainous landscape, which requires that the tea be harvested by hand, constitutes a permanent guarantee of quality.

ASSAM

The daily harvesting routine of the women in the upper Assam valley is similar to that of their Darjeeling counterparts, except for a few important details related to differences in climate and geography. The valley is one hundred and twenty miles to the east of Darjeeling, on the border of China, Burma and Bangladesh. At this longitude, the banks of the Brahmaputra (where wild tea plants sixty feet high were discovered in 1823) are among the wettest and least hospitable regions of the world. The valley, hidden between the Himalayas and Mounts Naga and Patkoi, was still overlaid with dense jungle growth when English colonists decided to clear it in the nineteenth century. It remains one of India's least-populated regions, and the mountains are inhabited by tribes whose way of life has not changed for thousands of years.

From April to September, the monsoon unleashes a torrent on the upper Assam valley that swells the river and floods the Ganges delta to the south, in Bangladesh. Every year, these floods take a heavy toll in human life. During the monsoon the temperature rises to 95° Farenheit. It is in this huge, natural greenhouse that nearly a third of Indian tea flourishes, yielding roughly two hundred thousand tons per year, including some of the finest varieties in the world.

Assamese pluckers do not resemble the Darjeeling mountain women. Rather, they are like other women on the Indian subcontinent, with large black eyes and delicate features. Although the image presented by the Tea Board of India shows smiling women in colorful saris and silver bracelets, the realities of climate and vegetation in fact impose particularly difficult working conditions on them.

They harvest eight hours per day in the atmosphere of an overheated greenhouse, and often have to don plastic bags to ward off insect and snake bites. After an overseer has given them the day's instructions on plots to be worked, and indicated assembly and weighing points, the women hoist a large wicker basket on their backs, held in place by a strap around the forehead. Then they advance by rows into one of Assam's two thousand gardens.

It might be Rungagora, Betjan, Silonibari or Keylung. It runs as far as the eye can see, over a stretch of one thousand acres, under large shade trees giving the appearance of a spacious, calm forest. Several hundred women work the garden every day, reaching nearly a thousand pluckers at the height of production between July and September.

In Asia, men are rarely seen harvesting

The upper Assam valley, in northeastern India, is the world's largest tea-producing region. Its two thousand gardens account for almost a third of India's annual harvest of seven hundred thousand tons. Yet it was not until the early twentieth century that the jungle along the banks of the Brahmaputra River, where wild tea plants grew in the torrential monsoon rains, was finally cleared. *Opposite:* The Mituoni plantation, with large shade trees reminiscent of a forest setting, is typical of the huge Assam gardens that sometimes extend over two thousand acres.

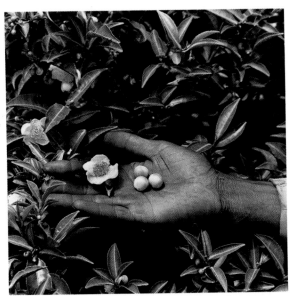

tea. It is generally said that the smallness, agility and patience of feminine hands are required for high-yield plucking with no loss in quality. Of course, it is more likely that sociological, economic and even symbolic reasons are behind this tradition, which some people feel contributes to the mysterious charm of tea. Whatever the case, picking tea on a grand estate requires specific skills, particularly dexterity. The women move between the tea plants—small shrubs spaced roughly thirty inches apart, regularly pruned to a height of four feet. With amazing swiftness and accuracy, they gather, with both hands, only the youngest, topmost leaves (which extend above the plane known as the "marker") by snapping the stem with a sharp movement of the index and middle fingers.

A "fine plucking" of the best teas removes only the terminal bud on the stem—covered with a fine white down—accompanied by the two first leaves below it. Most common teas are produced from a "coarse plucking" that includes the bud and three, four or even five leaves. But in all gardens, the pickers, in an age-old gesture, toss fistfuls of leaves over their shoulders into their baskets. This simple movement acquires the quality of an exploit when one realizes that in Assam, for example, each plucker harvests nearly fifty thousand stems per day. Once the basket is full, the pickers return in procession to an assembly point where the leaves are rapidly inspected and weighed. Pluckers are paid according to the

Plucking is a crucial operation that determines the ultimate quality of the brew. It requires a great deal of dexterity and care. The highest grade of top-quality tea is the product of a "fine plucking" in which only the terminal leaf-bud and first two leaves are picked. *Above:* Picking tea at Blue Mountains, a plantation in southern India. *Opposite, top:* A Bangladeshi woman at work. *Opposite, bottom:* The bud and two leaves harvested during a "fine plucking."

weight and quality of their harvest, generally several rupees (roughly a dollar) per day. Each cup of tea includes its measure of toil.

CEYLON

Milder breezes, lighter, clearer air and a rolling landscape lend the gardens of Ceylon a more pleasant mien. The brightly colored saris scattered among the greenery provide an appropriate touch of beauty. Things exist on a more human scale here, with estates sometimes as small as fifty acres. Most of them are located in the southwestern part of the island. The best gardens are, as always, found at the higher altitudes, from three thousand to eight thousand feet, on the eastern and western slopes of the high plateaus. Depending on the direction in which they face, the gardens are influenced by one of two monsoons; on the eastern slopes, the finest tea is plucked from late June to the end of August, whereas on the western slopes the best harvesting takes place from February 1st to March 15th.

It is now midday at Dimbula or Uva Highlands, Devonia or perhaps Pettiagalla. Tamil women in saris—or rather *lungis*,

Hugh Johnson pointed out that just as the Romans brought vineyards to the countries they conquered, so the English planted tea in India, Ceylon and Africa. *Above:* A garden in Ceylon with its factory and terraced slopes. *Opposite:* A colorful swirl of saris among shade trees in an Indian tea garden.

here—wear a long white cloth on their head to protect their shoulders from the sun. Despite their poverty, they sport silver bracelets, anklets, and gold necklaces. Their graceful and fragile silhouettes, slightly stooped, blend well with the tall tea plants left to grow like trees every thirty feet or so to provide a little shade and mark out the plots. Here and there, men dressed all in white—turban, jacket and long skirt down to their ankles—supervise the plucking. And when the baskets are full, they follow the pluckers to the door of the factory, where the tea is weighed. This tea factory in Ceylon, a long white building occupying the end of a small valley, looks somewhat like an Alpine sanatorium mistakenly set in the tropics. Although the soul of a garden resides in the hands of the pluckers, the factory represents both its heart and brain.

The black teas produced in Ceylon, India and China are the preferred teas in Europe and America. The freshly picked leaves undergo a long process of transformation, for black tea must be fermented. And the fermentation of tea requires as much care and close, scientifically controlled attention as does the fermentation of wine. This industrial

Throughout Asia, picking tea is women's work. It has long been said that only women have the patience and dexterity required for this delicate task. *Above:* Pluckers arrive at an estate in Ceylon's high-altitude Nuwara Eliya district. The long bamboo sticks sometimes used in gardens are placed horizontally at a given height, known as the "marker," indicating the level below which leaves are not to be picked. *Opposite:* Sorting leaves in Ceylon, prior to bagging and weighing them.

art constitutes the modern, technological face of these exotic and apparently unchanging tea gardens, and merits the same detailed description as the colorful swirl of saris. But whereas it is pleasant to linger under a shade tree to watch the plucking, ears lightly humming with the music of wind in leaves or the voices and murmured songs of the pickers, once at the door of the factory it becomes impossible to tarry for long—much less daydream—in the thundering din of machines.

Here, men do most of the work. Barefoot laborers and technicians in British-style shorts bustle among an indescribable clutter of machines, amid dim shade, heat and incessant noise.

Everywhere it is produced, black tea undergoes five successive stages. The leaves are first softened by a withering process that reduces their moisture content by half and enables them to be rolled without breaking. They are spread in thin layers on wide screens stacked eight inches apart to allow a current of warm air to circulate for roughly twenty-four hours. The most modern factories, however, now accomplish the task in tunnels or vats, reducing withering time to six hours.

Withering is followed by rolling (or maceration). The leaves are rolled to break down cell walls and release their essential oils. This was once done in the palm of the hand, but has long since been performed by impressive rolling machines composed of heavy metal disks rotating in opposite directions.

The rolled leaves are then placed on long mats to be sorted according to size and condition—whole or broken. This sorting is still done entirely by hand in some gardens, enabling the leaves to be "graded" into various classes of black tea. In the finest gardens, whole

Each stage in the production of tea takes place within the confines of the estate, from the carefully monitored sprouting of new plants in the nursery to the final packing of leaves ready for consumption. *Preceding double page:* Nursery at the Sangsua garden in Assam. New plants are increasingly being produced from cuttings rather than seedlings. *Above:* A garden in the Nilgiri district in southwestern India. Leaves are aired during the first stage of processing, known as withering, which slightly dries and softens them so that they can then be rolled without breaking. *Opposite:* A basket of freshly picked tea is carried into the factory at Glenloch Tea Estate, central Ceylon.

leaves are classified according to size and the way in which they are rolled, yielding Orange Pekoe (O.P., leaves rolled lengthwise and measuring from eight to fifteen millimeters), Flowery Orange Pekoe (F.O.P., leaves rolled in the same way yet smaller, from five to eight millimeters), Golden Flowery Orange Pekoe (G.F.O.P., an F.O.P. in which certain leaves have a golden tip), or Tippy Golden Flowery Orange Pekoe (T.G.F.O.P., all tips are golden). Leaves that have been broken, deliberately or not, yield high-quality grades of Broken Orange Pekoe (B.O.P.), Golden Broken Orange Pekoe (G.B.O.P.), or Tippy Golden Broken Orange Pekoe (T.G.B.O.P.). Finally, the so-called "crushed" leaves, which are in fact small pieces, are called Dust (less than one millimeter) and Fannings (one and a half millimeters).

Next comes fermentation, the crucial operation that endows black tea with its color and, above all, the subtlety of its flavor. Experts agree that the process remains something of a mystery. No one knows exactly what alchemy produces the flavors, for certain cellular reactions during fermentation have never been fully understood or even identified. We do know that fermentation is produced by exposing leaves to a highly moist atmosphere (at least 90 percent humidity) after having been spread on broad slabs of cement, glass or aluminum. The air temperature must be carefully monitored and controlled (between 72° and 82° F), because a slight rise in temperature will give the tea a burned taste, whereas a slight drop will halt fermentation. When maintained at constant temperature and humidity, the leaf first heats up from the effect of several chemical reactions, then begins to cool off. A tea-maker's skill includes an adept sense of timing—for best results, fermentation should be halted just when the leaf stops heating, which may take from one to three hours.

The leaves are then dried in an enormous machine comprising a dryer and conveyor belt, exposing them to temperatures of at least 175° F for roughly twenty minutes. Drying, the last stage of transformation, also requires well-honed skills. If it is too brief, the tea may become moldy in time; too long, and the tea will lose much of its flavor. All this expertise goes into the black tea that emerges from the great gardens of Asia.

The Tamil pluckers continue to work into the afternoon, repeating the morning's tasks. Meanwhile, several thousand miles away in Africa, on the jungle-covered slopes of Mount Cameroon and the high plateaus of Kenya, dawn is breaking over other gardens that produce several unique varieties of black tea. Here it is men who rise early to pluck the tea planted in the red soil among eucalyptus trees. British planters who left India following independence found favorable climatic conditions in the higher altitudes of Africa. It is said that the chocolate aroma of Broken

Producing black tea requires five successive operations. After the tea is withered, it is macerated (or "rolled")—the leaves are rolled or crushed to release essential oils. Leaves are then sorted according to size and form (whole or broken leaf). The next operation is the fermentation, which transforms green leaves into black tea; the leaves are spread in thin layers and exposed to warm, humid air at a constant temperature for several hours. The final stage entails drying (or "firing") the leaves to halt fermentation. *Opposite:* Tea being fermented at Glenloch Tea Estate, in the mountains of Ceylon.

Three of the stages in the production process—rolling, sorting and firing—were mechanized in the 1880s. *Above:* Once picked, the leaves are set out to wither, then placed in rolling and drying machines. *Opposite:* Inside a factory near Ootacamund, in southern India.

Orange Pekoe Fannings (B.O.P.F.) produced on Mount Cameroon became a favorite of the court of England.

CHINA

Although the English taste for black tea taken with sugar and a drop of milk has become the European norm, the vast majority of Asians and North Africans prefer the original green tea that has been consumed in China for over five thousand years. The gardens producing the finest green tea are found on continental China, on Formosa, and in Japan. In China, tea is still made using methods employed from time immemorial. In artisanal cooperative factories, the tea is first steamed for less than a minute in large vats, in order to kill the fermentation enzymes that would otherwise subsequently alter its quality. Next it is kneaded by hand, stacked in small piles, and dried for approximately ten hours, during which time it is regularly turned. The tea is then rolled according to the desired grade, and finally sorted. In Japan and Formosa, these operations are now mechanized. The grades into which green tea is sorted include Gunpowder, used for the finest mint teas in North Africa and the Near East (leaves rolled into tiny balls from one to three millimeters in diameter), Chun-Mee (rolled leaves one centimeter long), Sencha (whole, unrolled leaves, also called "Natural Leaf"), and Matcha (powdered tea used in Japan for the tea ceremony).

No visitor ever set foot in the very best Chinese gardens, which remain shrouded in mystery. Few Chinese even know that these gardens exist, for they are familiar only with the state cooperatives that produce "standard" black and green teas identified by number and skillfully blended to guarantee stable quality whatever the climatic conditions. Certain standard teas are nonetheless high-quality products designed mainly for export, such as Imperial Yunnan from the high plateaus of southern China, or the sweet Imperial Keemun from the mountains of Anhui province. China's secret gardens, however, are kept distinct from these cooperatives, and are called "sacred gardens" by the privileged few. Their exact number—perhaps three or four—is unknown. They are said to be patrolled day and night by police dogs. Why such secrecy? Surely because these gardens produce tiny quantities of superlative green tea that is kept off the market and reserved exclusively for high government officials.

Halfway between the cooperatives and the sacred gardens, China also has gardens producing tea that can be purchased, assuming that one has managed to establish a special relationship with certain authorities. These gardens in the mountainous regions of Sichuan (Szechwan) and Jiangsu yield some of the finest, rarest and of course most expensive

Legend has it that tea was discovered in China five thousand years ago when a tea leaf fell into the bowl of Emperor Shen Nung, seated beneath a wild tea plant. The Chinese plant, which is the hardiest variety, has made China the birthplace of the tea industry. In recent years, the Chinese have discovered numerous giant tea trees growing wild in the country's unexplored southern regions. One of them, over one hundred feet high and with a trunk over three feet in diameter, has been growing in a primitive forest in Yunnan for seventeen hundred years.

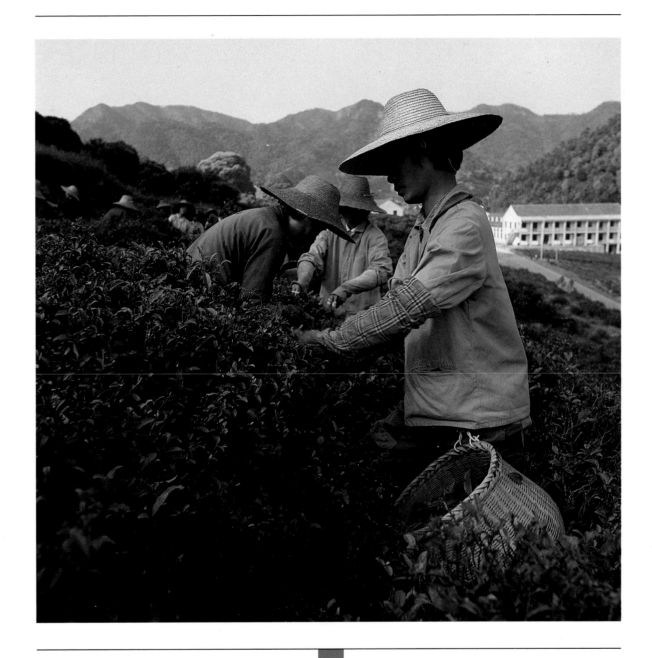

In modern-day China, true "gardens" are both rare and secret. Most black and green tea is produced on huge state cooperatives, then marketed in the form of numbered teas of guaranteed standard and quality. Certain outstanding teas are nevertheless given special names. *Above:* Pluckers at work in a cooperative near Hangzhou in Zhejiang province, known for its famous Lung Ching ("Dragon Well"), one of the world's finest green teas.

green teas in the world. Such teas are called Pi Lo Chun ("Spiral of Spring Jade") and Lung Ching ("Dragon's Well"). Yet even these teas seem somewhat ordinary compared to a tea practically worth its weight in gold. This is not a green tea, but white (not steamed, merely dried), a veritable miracle produced in Fujian province known as Yin Zhen ("Silver Needles"). This garden is one of the very few plantations still in existence, almost all of them located on the high China plateaus, that still practice the traditional plucking method formerly reserved for the emperor and a few court dignitaries. Known as "imperial plucking," this method removes only the bud and the first leaf from the bush. Sometimes, as with Yin Zhen, only the bud itself is picked. In the past, nothing was permitted to alter the purity of the plant from the time it was plucked to the moment it reached the emperor's bowl.

Young virgins, gloved and using gold scissors, delicately clipped the stem and placed it in a golden basket, where the leaves were dried prior to being placed in the imperial bowl. No one knows what precautions are taken today to preserve the incredibly subtle aroma of "silver needles," which reminds the most sophisticated palates of the fragrance of orchids. All that is known is that the tea is plucked only once a year, during two days selected according to minute botanical observations. Should unanticipated wind or rain arrive during those two days, the annual harvest is purely and simply canceled.

FORMOSA

China offers no glimpse of its sacred gardens, nor does it like to show its large estates to foreigners. Moreover, these plantations often

In the People's Republic of China, mists and fog often compensate for insufficient rainfall, at the same time cloaking the gardens in secrecy. Here tea is produced according to ancient, time-tested methods, and workers perform all tasks by hand, just like their ancestors. *Above:* A plantation on the island of Hainan, to the south of the mainland. *Opposite:* A plucker in Szechwan, one of the six main tea-producing regions in China.

remain veiled in mists or, as in Fujian province, hidden behind screens of smoke from the spruce pine that yields its fragrance to Lapsang Souchong before wafting from the factory chimney. The smoke only clears sixty miles to the east, in the sky over the strait of Formosa, off the coast of Taiwan. Here, in full view and to the great delight of demanding tea-lovers from Hong Kong and Singapore, the great Chinese teas of yore are being reborn. Rich merchants, bankers and shipping magnates now buy extravagantly expensive green tea in Formosa, tea harvested and produced in small family gardens with artisanal methods, exactly as it was done in imperial China. Approximately one hundred families thus produce Oolong, the island's great specialty, a so-called "semifermented" tea because it undergoes only an initial stage of fermentation. Its taste and color are halfway between green tea and black tea.

This one-day, whirlwind tour of the world's finest tea gardens reaches northern Formosa in the afternoon. Here, in a small mountain chain, a superior semifermented tea known as Ti Kuan Yin ("The Goddess") is grown. It is reputed to eliminate all impurities from the body. Formosa benefits from an ideal climate for growing tea—very humid, with temperatures never rising above 82° F in summer yet never dropping below 55° F in winter. The harvest lasts eight months, from April to November. Mr. Chang, a small independent tea-grower, displays medals won during the annual Ti Kuan Yin contest on the rustic walls of his office. Through the window, pluckers can be seen working in the mist. Like all the best Formosa teas, Mr. Chang's Ti Kuan Yin is not available through normal export channels involving brokers, telexes or commodity exchanges where tea is auctioned to importers the world over. Any foreign buyer who wants Mr. Chang's tea must go straight to the grower, at least the first time. If the buyer is lucky, the wind will disperse the mist for a moment or two, and the lofty gardens of Ti Kuan Yin will offer a vantage point from which to contemplate the entire north end of the island, from Taipei to the sea twelve miles away.

JAPAN

This tour of the world's tea gardens in fact provides a good opportunity to survey some impressive landscapes, to surrender to the fascination of endless vistas, enigmatic mists, gargantuan mountains. For thousands of years, the landscape in which tea is grown—so propitious to contemplation and meditation—has brought mankind closer to the heavens, if not the gods. It is probably no coincidence that it was a Buddhist monk named Saichô, a member of the Tendai sect, who first brought tea plants to Japan from China early in the ninth century. Three or four hundred years later, Zen monks would

Tea cultivation was introduced into Japan in the ninth century by a Buddhist monk. To this day, tea remains an integral part of Japanese spiritual life. Thus the magnificent gardens dotting the islands seem specifically designed to encourage meditation, like Zen rock gardens. *Opposite:* Motionless waves of tea in a garden in the Shizuoka district to the west of Tokyo, where most of Japan's green tea is grown.

drink a large bowl of Matcha, a powdered green tea rich in vitamins, in order to perform long hours of meditation without flagging. In Japan, tea began and then spread as an accompaniment to spiritual exercise. So it is hardly surprising that the nation's tea gardens are works of art

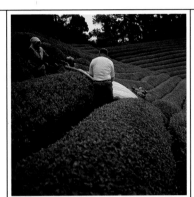

as sublime as Zen rock gardens, even if they do not necessarily have the same symbolic import.

Japanese tea gardens are unlike any others. It is sometimes hard to believe that tea is being grown on them. From a distance, they look like vast stretches of some vivid green liquid that veils the hills, frozen into motionless waves. This effect is due to the way the bushes are planted and pruned; they are not spaced apart, as elsewhere, but are placed sided by side to form lengthy, tight strips thirty yards long, whose uniform and slightly curved surface forms an enormous plucking table. All these strips are identical in size, planted in parallel rows roughly a yard apart, perpendicular to the slope. Except perhaps in Java or Bali, with their terraced rice fields, no other growers have managed to sculpt the land so beautifully. But everyone knows that, in Japan, the functional is inevitably beautiful.

Japan produces only green tea, known as O-Cha. It is grown in the Mount Fuji area, on the island of Kyushu, and in Shizuoka, the main growing region known for its infinite variety of the most common tea, Sencha. In winter, hot-air fans protect the tea plants from the threat of frost.

The afternoon wanes delightfully in the Uji countryside, near Kyoto, where natural springs spill down the finely carved emerald hills. In the garden, women in long red aprons glide slowly between the motionless waves. They pluck what some people consider the finest green tea on the planet—Gyokuro, "Precious Dew." Nowhere else (except, perhaps, in China's sacred gardens) is tea cultivated with such care. Three weeks before the harvest, as soon as the first buds appear, the entire plantation is covered with mats of bamboo, reed or dark canvas to filter out 90 percent of the light. The tiny leaves that grow in the semi-darkness thus have a higher chlorophyll content (hence the emerald green color) and a lower tannin content (rendering the tea less bitter). Gyokuro is the mellowest of green teas. Like the rare teas of China, it is harvested only once each year, in late April or early May, according to the imperial method that removes only the bud and, if quality allows, the first leaf. Once reduced to powder, the

In characteristic Japanese fashion, sophisticated technology coexists with centuries-old tradition. Gardens are sometimes heated in winter by electric radiators, and harvesting machines move through rows of tea plants without diminishing the quality of the finished product. *Above:* Mechanical harvesting at a Shizuoka garden. *Opposite:* Traditional wicker baskets filled with tea leaves. Green (that is to say, unfermented) tea, the only kind produced in Japan, is made by steaming the leaves, then drying and rolling them. To obtain the Matcha tea used in the tea ceremony, the leaves are pulverized into a powder.

precious tea from this garden becomes Matcha Uji, the most subtle of Matcha teas, used in the traditional Japanese tea ceremony.

TEAS THE WORLD OVER

India, Ceylon, China, Formosa, Japan, Cameroon and Kenya are not the only countries with fine tea gardens. Some of the other twenty-three tea-growing countries also offer high-quality specialty teas. Indonesia, for instance, boasts Java Taloon, although this variety may not long withstand the drive for profitability now sweeping the islands, spurring growers to produce ordinary teas for teabag consumption. Sikkim, a small Indian protectorate in the Himalayas, produces a Temi rivaling the best Darjeelings. Nepal, with its Everest plantations, also produces fine tea.

In other countries, where intensive and fully mechanized production methods are used, there are no "gardens." In parts of the former Soviet Union, once the world's fourth largest producer, machines straddle hedges of tea bushes planted as far as the eye can see in the plains of Georgia, the Caucasus, and Azerbaijan. Such tea is satisfactory for everyday use, but not for the sophisticated palates of certain privileged officials who pay a fortune for the finest Darjeelings on the Colombo exchange in Ceylon. (Colombo employs a reverse auction system—a maximum price is announced, and the first bidder to match or to come closest to that price carries the lot. In the two other major international exchanges, London and Calcutta, dozens of brokers buy and sell the finest teas according to a conventional auction system.) Turkey and Iran in the Near East, Brazil and Argentina in South America, and Tanzania, Malawi and Uganda in Africa also produce average-quality teas usually destined for teabags.

The tour returns to Darjeeling as evening falls. In the nursery of a garden such as Singtom or Selimbong, technicians monitor the growth of young *Camellia sinensis* plants. These cuttings are raised for two or three years under a shelter of woven branches. When they are nearly two feet high, they are planted in the garden.

Not far away, in a well-lit room at the factory where the machines have just fallen silent, a hundred white porcelain cups—filled with infused tea and topped with a cover—are lined up on a large table. Each is placed between an empty bowl and a small vessel filled with dry

The large international tea exchange in Colombo, Ceylon during a power failure.
Unfazed, the tea brokers continue to trade by candlelight.

tea. A man pours the contents of the cups into the bowls, through the sieved cover that stops the leaves. This cover, full of steeped leaves, is then turned upward. Once the operation has been completed, the garden's official taster examines the dry leaves, the steeped leaves, and the color of the liquid in the bowl. He sniffs the tea, tastes it, then spits it out in a large basin that he pushes before him as he goes along. He makes notes in a heavy ledger. Every day during the harvest, prior to packing, the produce of each plot in the garden is subjected to this quality-control tasting.

Prior to reaching retail shops all across the world, the finest teas will be tasted in this way at least four more times. Once by the broker (or his taster) who then sends samples to importers. And then three more times by the importing expert, who then places orders with the broker. Another tasting takes place after the tea has been bought at auction (in Colombo or Calcutta), just prior to shipping, to verify that the bulk product corresponds to the original sample. A final tasting occurs when the tea has reached its port of destination, to make sure that shipping has not affected quality. Naturally, these multiple tastings are not performed on "standard" China teas (due to predictable quality), nor on the ordinary teas used in most blends.

The day-long tour draws to a close. It has now been several hours since the pluckers left Darjeeling's gardens. Tea harvested the day before has just been packed in chests whose corners are sealed shut with aluminum plaques. As the sun sets, enormous pink and black clouds appear over the mountains. The wind murmurs through the leaves, barely disturbing the silence. The soil in the garden, depleted by the long day, awaits the rain.

This chapter was written with the expert assistance of Mariage Frères tea dealers, Paris.

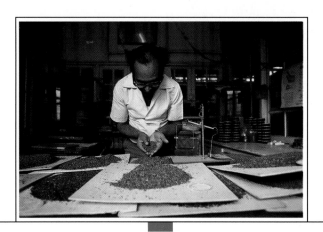

The day draws to a close in the tea gardens. *Above:* The tasting room of a factory in southern India's Nilgiri district, where teas similar to those from Ceylon are grown. A tea maker prepares a subtle blend of leaves that were plucked the preceding day, and which have just emerged from the dryer. *Opposite:* This blend being packed in chests is a green gunpowder tea, the basis of the finest mint teas consumed in North Africa.

· TIME ·

FOR TEA

Gilles Brochard

More tea is drunk, worldwide, than any other beverage—except water. From China to England, from India to America, and from Japan to Morocco, tea has acquired a vast multitude of followers, leaving its mark on every civilization. Each day, over one and a half *billion* cups of tea are consumed on the planet. This success is due to the fact that tea has been able to adapt itself to the cultures it has encountered. For, unlike modern soft drinks that sweep across the planet with the help of colossal advertising campaigns, tea has never been perceived as a threat to a way of life, has never been synonymous with uniformity. It is not generally a ready-made beverage consumed straight from a can or bottle. To the contrary, tea requires a sometimes lengthy rite of preparation, stimulating an inventiveness that is conducive to the free expression of individual tastes. Many different attitudes and cultures are thus encountered along the route that leads from a steaming bowl of *cha* with yak butter to a tall glass of iced tea with lemon, from ceremonial Matcha to *thé au lait*.

CHINA, BIRTHPLACE OF TEA

Ever since its lucky "discovery" by Emperor Chen Nung in 2737 B.C. (a leaf from a wild tea plant reportedly fell into his bowl of hot water), the first three thousand years in the history of tea were a purely and intensely

Above: A French advertisement for "mandarin-flavored China tea" (probably a scented blend), circa 1900. *Opposite:* A photo taken from *The English at Home*, a photo essay created in the 1930s by the famous photographer Bill Brandt. *Page 100:* Tea break at a London factory, circa 1930. During the Depression, employers resisted the idea of a tea break, but British labor unions made it a bargaining issue alongside wage demands.

Chinese affair. In *The Chinese Art of Tea,* John Blofeld noted that every layer of Chinese society played a part in this history, including "emperors and peasants, Taoist recluses, Buddhist monks, wandering physicians, mandarins (the scholar-officials of old China), lovely ladies, craftsmen, potters, poets, singers, painters, architects, landscape gardeners, nomadic tribesmen who bartered horses for bricks of tea, and statesmen who used tea to buy off would-be invaders. . . ."

Even though China, unlike Japan, never transformed the drinking of tea into a sacred ceremony, it nevertheless initiated the time-honored ritual of offering a bowl of tea to a guest as a sign of welcome. This tradition was reportedly begun by a disciple of Lao Tse named Kuanyin who one day offered the "old philosopher" a cup of the golden elixir. Thus by 500 B.C., tea had become what it remains today in many countries, especially in Asia—a mark of friendship and hospitality. Once associated with Taoist philosophy and therefore intimately linked to the rise of Zen Buddhism, tea was also thought to provide the energy required for meditation.

But it was not until the flamboyant T'ang dynasty (A.D. 618-907) that tea, long drunk and appreciated for its medicinal properties, became an object both of veneration and flourishing trade. Highly prized at court, it acquired followers throughout the empire, winning converts in Tibet and among nomad-ic peoples living beyond China's northern and western borders, such as the Mongols, Turks and Tatars. The shrewd imperial government profited from this infatuation by taxing the tea trade. During the same period, the poet Lu Yu composed a paean to tea in the form of the *Chaking,* the first history of tea. Generations of tea dealers subsequently worshiped Lu Yu as a sort of patron saint. He inspired numerous disciples, including Lu T'ung, nicknamed the "tea maniac." Lu T'ung was a Taoist poet born at the end of the eighth century who lived aloof from the world, in Hunan, where he became one of the first "tea masters." Venerated by his contemporaries, Lu T'ung devoted his life to poetry and the preparation of tea, occupations summed up in a now famous line of poetry: "I am in no way interested in immortality, but only in the taste of tea."

Under the T'ang dynasty, tea was glorified by poets and codified by tea masters, becoming the quintessential beverage of refined souls. The art of pottery also made great advances during this period, evolving toward more sophisticated forms and techniques. Teapots and bowls in engraved gold and silver even came into use until tea masters categorically forbade the use of metallic utensils. Tea was usually drunk in large wooden bowls. Water was boiled in terracotta vessels, and the tea itself came in the form of leaves, powder or cakes. Connoisseurs

"Everywhere in Chinese towns one encounters large shops where people go solely to drink tea. These shops house square wooden tables around which are placed benches and chairs. In the back is the laboratory . . . stocked with countertops carrying enormous kettles and huge teapots." William Milne, *La Vie réelle en Chine,* 1850. *Below:* A nineteenth-century teapot in red clay, from Yixing. *Opposite, top:* The Woo Sing Ding shop in Shanghai, circa 1900, that reportedly inspired the so-called "willow-tree pattern" used on English porcelain. *Opposite, bottom:* Tea house in Nanking, circa 1930.

preferred it in this latter form, for it could be broken into larger or smaller pieces that were crushed into powder prior to preparation.

The art of tea reached its height from the tenth century onward, under the Song dynasty, also famous for its pottery. In order to obtain the finest tea, everyone sought to perfect each stage of preparation. The quality of the water, the quality of the tea plant, and especially the type of utensil (like the little grinder used to crush tea leaves or the cleft bamboo stick used to stir the water) took on considerable importance in the eyes of tea-lovers. The wooden bowls used during the T'ang era were replaced by larger, shallower vessels called *chien*. Soon tea contests became fashionable, notably among highly placed government officials. Zealots would jealously keep their brewing techniques secret, going so far as to travel alone to seek water from a preferred mountain spring.

Emperor Hui Tsun (1100-1126) encouraged this search for perfection, even complaining of the "waste of so much good tea through improper handling." As painter, poet and playboy who delighted in the company of courtesans, the emperor was sometimes criticized for placing pleasure over duty. But everyone recognized his expertise at preparing tea, and the emperor's treatise on tea, *Ta Kuan Ch'a Lun*, became the connoisseurs' bible. The book praised the virtues of a drink that freed the mind from stress, both physical and mental, thus making it possible to forget the world for an instant and attain total serenity. The emperor's own serenity required a particularly pure form of tea. The "imperial plucking" method obeyed strict rules and was used only for the emperor's tea: the leaves were picked

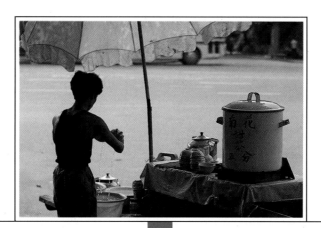

The jasmine tea usually served in Chinese restaurants in the West is falsely exotic, since the Chinese themselves do not drink tea during meals. In fact, they do not drink anything during meals, except on special occasions when alcoholic toasts are offered. Tea is nevertheless widely consumed between meals, all day long. It may be drunk in the street (where traditional hawkers still sell it) or at the office (thanks to enamel thermos bottles). *Above and opposite:* Street hawkers in Canton today, and in a village of the past. *Preceding double page:* A nineteenth-century painting illustrates two ways of serving tea—a teapot and ordinary cups can be seen on the table in the back, whereas the servant carries covered cups in which tea is brewed directly.

inese Hawker

by young virgins wearing gloves and using gold scissors; they cut only the bud and the youngest leaf, which were left on a golden platter to dry before being poured directly into the emperor's bowl.

Not all Chinese could aspire to such a degree of purity. In Hangzhou, the Song capital in southern China, high-ranked civil servants gathered in tea houses known for their luxury, their warmth, their magnificent floral decorations and calligraphed scrolls, and their excellent "plum flower" alcohol accompanied by delicacies—not to mention the music lessons also given there. Less wealthy tea-lovers generally called on the services of street hawkers. But they could also go to working-class tea houses that Marco Polo felt were of dubious propriety, since somewhat bawdy ladies enlivened the atmosphere with song.

Following a long period of conflict sparked by the Mongol invasion and subsequent rebellion against the heavy taxation imposed by the invaders (tea not being exempt from the general hike in tribute demanded), China slowly returned to stability with the Ming dynasty, founded in 1368 at Nanking. The production of tea increased and techniques evolved—old-fashioned bottles for boiling tea were replaced by kettles and, since it was no longer conceivable to drink tea "like some thirsty ox," rustic wooden bowls were replaced by tiny cups of fine porcelain. Tea leaves were no longer boiled and stirred, but merely steeped, which meant that the teapot became the most important utensil in preparing the beverage.

This typically Chinese method of steeping tea soon found followers on another continent. Tea and China porcelain arrived in Europe at the beginning of the seventeenth century on Dutch East India Company ships. At the same time, the use of tea leaves spread across Japan and Korea, countries that had consumed tea in powdered form until that point. In Korea, where by the eighth century the art of tea was as refined as in China, a little ginseng was often added to the brew.

As the centuries passed, tea became a staple in China, along with salt, rice and vinegar. Up until the 1950s, people from all walks of life drank tea during the day, whether at home, in tea houses, or at work. In private homes, the tradition of offering tea to guests—even unexpected ones—was upheld. Tea was kept hot in large teapots nestled in quilted baskets. It was not unusual for a storekeeper to offer customers a bowl of tea, and tea was often made available to hotel guests in their rooms. In cities from Peking to Canton, tea houses opened at dawn to welcome those who, an hour after sunrise—the moment when vital energy is at its purest—would be out strolling with their caged pet birds. These early customers would be followed by tradesmen, apprentices, and

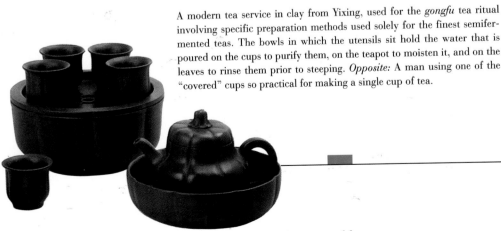

A modern tea service in clay from Yixing, used for the *gongfu* tea ritual involving specific preparation methods used solely for the finest semifermented teas. The bowls in which the utensils sit hold the water that is poured on the cups to purify them, on the teapot to moisten it, and on the leaves to rinse them prior to steeping. *Opposite:* A man using one of the "covered" cups so practical for making a single cup of tea.

workers. In tea-producing regions, villagers liked to gather in the finest tea houses in the world, those in the midst of the plantations, near a pure mountain spring.

John Blofeld, who spent thirty years in China, described a student picnic that he attended in the hills north of Chongqing just after the Second World War. The fire was fanned with a dry banana leaf that replaced the "broken fan" usually employed for such rustic operations. The tea was prepared on a charcoal stove. Each guest drank four bowls of green tea. Then an unusual game began, in which Blofeld participated. The game involved composing a poem on a given subject—the spring water. Blofeld mumbled a few words on the theme, in English, and his poem was submitted to general criticism. Fortunately, his honor was not impugned and the "true spirit of tea" prevailed.

Although tea is still drunk at home in China, most of the tea houses disappeared during the "cultural revolution," along with traditional tea celebrations and the drinking of tea in public. The art of making tea and relaxing over a cup was designated as an "unproductive leisure activity," and therefore practically forbidden. China has nevertheless pursued a policy of massive exportation and carefully cultivates its "sacred gardens," small plantations where the imperial plucking method is secretly employed to supply top government officials with the finest green and white teas in the world.

In recent years, however, some tea houses have begun to re-open, such as the Red Lantern in Chengdu, where storytellers bring Chinese feudal traditions back to life.

For the Muslim population in Kashi, the largest urban agglomeration in western China, tea-drinking traditions bear little resemblance to Chinese customs but are more closely related to those of the caravan routes beyond the border. *Above:* In Kashi, after men leave the Id Kah mosque following the Friday prayer, women solemnly offer them bread and tea. *Opposite:* Famous teas rooms in Shanghai (Xu Xing Ting, *top*, Mandarin Garden, *center*) and in Macao (Loc Koc, *bottom*).

THE WAY OF TEA

A disciple of Sen Rikyû, the great tea master, once asked, "Can you tell me exactly what, above all, must be understood and kept in mind during a tea ceremony?" The master answered: "Make a delicious bowl of tea; arrange the charcoal to heat the water; arrange the flowers the way they are in the fields; in summer, suggest coolness, in winter, warmth; anticipate everything; be ready for rain; show the greatest possible consideration toward your guests."

These few words express it all. In the sixteenth century, Rikyû codified the current tea ceremony, known as cha-no-yu (literally, "hot-water tea"). His advice, appreciated and faithfully followed by subsequent generations, was capped by a final comment. "Tea is nothing other than this: heat the water, prepare the tea and drink it with propriety. That is all you need to know."

The "Way of Tea" incarnates all the poetic beauty of Japanese spiritual philosophy. The ceremony is performed in a private tea house called the sukiya, which might be translated as the "Abode of Vacancy." As pointed out by Kakuzo Okakura in his 1906 Book of Tea, each celebrant knows that the ceremony is "more than an idealization of the form of drinking—it is a religion of the art of life." Celebrants should therefore religiously follow the strict rites established in the sixteenth century, a ritual inspired by Chinese Buddhist monks. The tea used is Matcha, or "froth of liquid jade," a powdered green tea that is not steeped but whipped in the bowl with a small bamboo whisk called a chasen.

Yasunari Kawabata wrote that "a tea ceremony is a communion of feeling, when good friends come together at the right moment, under the best conditions." The ceremony is by nature simple, yet codified down to the smallest detail. Prior to entering the "Abode of Fancy" or "Abode of Vacancy," guests must cross a garden by a path of paving stones, the roji ("earth damp with dew"). They walk silently, leaving worldly sounds behind. Trees, moss and bird-song help instill a mood of concentration. Establishing harmony with nature is an indispensable prelude to the ceremony, and it extends to the waiting room where several flowers are placed in a bamboo vase. Sometimes, prior to leaving the garden, the host (who has silently greeted his friends) invites his guests to perform the purification ritual of rinsing their mouths and washing their hands in a small stone basin.

The central room where the guests sit is decorated by a hanging scroll, parchment or painting, selected according to the day, the season, or theme of the gathering. The host enters via a sliding door, and serves a light, quintessentially Japanese meal, kaiseki, to

"As dusk gave way to the first stars, the women arrived, bowing delightfully. . . . Spicy pickled fruit was passed around on cleverly shaped trays. There then appeared transparent porcelain cups, the size of half an egg, from which the ladies drank a few drops of sugarless tea poured from doll-like kettles." Pierre Loti, Madame Chrysanthème. Opposite: Two engravings by Toshikata, dated 1905, from a series of prints on the tea ceremony—arranging accessories (top) and bidding farewell to the guests (bottom).

each of the guests seated cross-legged on mats. Each dish, served in simple yet refined crockery, comes from either the sea or the mountains. Food is to be savored in three ways, according to Soshitsu Sen—"with the eyes, the tongue, and the heart." Guests use freshly cut chopsticks of green bamboo, making the contact of food and mouth all the more pleasant. At the end of the meal, the host offers everyone a syrup-drenched cake or a delicacy made of white bean curd (*namagushi*). Guests may then get some fresh air in the garden, prior to sitting down once again to drink the strong tea.

The host carefully handles the required instruments—the teapot containing Matcha, the tea spoon, the *chasen*. Water is heated in a kettle placed on a charcoal stove sunk into the middle of the floor. Tradition demands that guests share the same bowl, each awaiting his or her turn. The host—who does not partake—patiently repeats the preparation, never forgetting to greet the person who extends his hands for the bowl. Guests must hold the bowl in both hands, with the porcelain pattern turned toward the host. The tea, with its fine avocado hue and slightly starchy taste, will be drunk in this way three times. Every object is then

conscientiously washed and put away in the alcove. Then the host returns and offers a cake to each guest, followed by weaker tea served in a different bowl. The tea ceremony concludes in silent contemplation of the fire and the surroundings. The host accompanies his friends to the threshold, then carefully puts away the utensils, removes the flowers and sees to the cleanliness and order of the tea house.

"In the eyes of an uninitiated observer," notes Soshitsu Sen, "nothing extraordinary happens. The host and his guest nevertheless expect this experience to constitute a microcosm of life itself." Learning to perform the tea ceremony requires long training, and Japanese children take lessons after school hours, just like music or dancing lessons. Instructors must serve long years of apprenticeship before becoming qualified masters. Women, whether or not they come from a family with a strong tea tradition, have been allowed to perform the ceremony since the beginning of the twentieth century if they receive the approval of a grand master.

Although the tea ceremony is still practiced today, it obviously encounters the complications that go with modern Japanese life. For it can only be performed inside

Felice Beato's photographs, taken in the 1860s, document Japanese traditions just prior to the industrialization and Westernization of the country. The prints were colored by hand, using a Japanese method then unknown in Europe, adding an unusual dimension to these scenes of everyday life in which tea seems to be a constant feature. *Above:* Guests at an inn. *Opposite:* Woman at her toilet, and a strolling street hawker.

The Urasenke Foundation in Kyoto is the most famous of the three Japanese schools of tea. *Above:* Inside the foundation, a gateway and *roji* (path of stones and pine needles) lead to the "tea room." *Opposite:* The tea master's house, and one of the rooms in which the "Way of Tea" is taught.

a private tea house made of specific materials, conforming to certain proportions, and set in a garden.

The mistress of an ordinary house may nevertheless perform the ceremony if a room is set aside for that purpose. She will invite her guests, in writing, three or four weeks in advance of the occasion, perhaps in honor of the arrival of a friend in town, or the blossoming of the cherry trees, or simply to admire the moon.

As to public tea houses, they had their moment of glory in Japan in the seventeenth century. They were true pleasure houses, where people bawled out songs and played music. They often had rooms where guests could spend the night.

Recent modernization—or rather, Americanization—has led to a drop in the consumption of tea in Japan, in favor of other beverages. Japanese green tea is drunk early in the morning to get a good start on the day, or before a meal to help digestion, thereby losing its sophistication and becoming an everyday drink. In the past ten years, the Japanese have tended to replace this leafy green tea first by semifermented tea and then, after a period of transition, by black tea that is sometimes sold in nylon teabags. The latest craze seems to be for scented blends and flavored tea (such as apple tea), often imported from France and therefore known locally as "French tea." True tea-lovers hope that the Japanese, and in particular Japanese youth, will gradually rediscover the "Way of Tea." For tea remains deeply etched in contemporary Japanese culture—it is the only country in the world to elect a

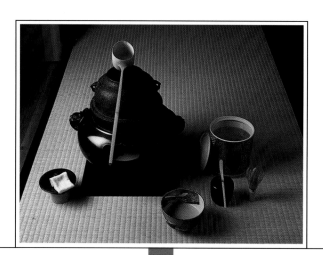

The great tea master Rikyû was suspected of having betrayed his lord, and was therefore obliged to commit suicide. He organized a final tea ceremony, at the end of which he broke his bowl with these words: "May this cup, soiled by the lips of misfortune, never serve another man." *Above:* Utensils employed in the tea ceremony, including the kettle and the ladle used to scoop water. *Opposite:* A craftsman makes the little whisk used to whip the mixture of water and powdered tea (Matcha).

"Miss Tea" each year to promote the year's harvest. Artists and filmmakers also often pay homage to the role of tea, as seen, for instance, in Yasujiro Ozu's film *The Bitter Flavor of Green Tea over Rice*.

TEA FROM TIBET AND INDIA

High on Himalayan pastures, shepherds occupying the mountain huts in springtime may well offer a passing traveler salted tea with goat's milk. This is common practice among Tibetans, who often replace the goat's milk with yak butter. Their green, salty tea is generally accompanied by the famous *tsamba*, a flat cake of ground parched barley or corn, mixed with buckwheat and kneaded into balls.

In the mid-nineteenth century, Father E. R. Huc's *Souvenirs d'un voyage dans la Tartarie, le Tibet et la Chine* included a description of ceremonial offerings of tea in Tibetan lamaseries. Huc noted that there were two types of "tea session"—the "special tea" given by a pilgrim for a small group of lamas, and the "general tea" that might be offered to over four thousand people gathered for a major celebration, thereby costing the generous donor a fortune. "On the appointed day of the offering of general tea . . . forty young *chabis*, chosen at random, went to the large kitchen and reappeared a moment later carrying large jars of tea with milk. They moved through the rows, and as they advanced the lamas drew their wooden bowls from their breasts. These were then filled to the brim.

When Alexandra David-Neel first arrived in India, she noted that "near the port was a pavilion where one could take tea, excellent tea, with toast, cakes and other products of English culinary art." *L'Inde où j'ai vécu*. India imitated this British ritual, modifying it to accommodate local traditions and even adopting certain Tibetan customs (such as steeping the leaves in milk). *Above:* On the Pakistani border, Indian soldiers drink tea accompanied by spicy pastries called *samosas*. *Opposite:* A Kashmiri woman takes a break from farm chores to drink tea flavored with cardamom seeds and crushed almonds.

Everyone drank in silence, taking care to draw the corner of a scarf in front of the bowl. This gesture of modesty was an acknowledgment of the unseemliness of this material act, so out of keeping with the holiness of the place. . . . When the celebration was over, the presiding lama solemnly pronounced the name of the pious pilgrim who had obtained the immense merit of entertaining the holy community of lamas."

Tibet is perhaps the only place in the world where tea is considered a sacred offering. Yet it is also an essential element of local hospitality, as in China. A guest will usually be invited to sit at a low table set before the hearth, that center of domestic life. The table will be set with a bowl, a *tsamba* box and sometimes a sort of churn used to mix the butter into the salty tea. To avoid bad luck, bowls must be filled to the brim.

A thousand years separate the ninth-century arrival of Chinese tea in Tibet and the nineteenth-century planting of Chinese tea in India by English colonists. India, notably the Himalayan foothills in the north, was a land highly suited to the cultivation of a shrub that already grew wild in the Assam region. Assam, in fact, produced the first Indian tea, which was sold in London in 1839. Living conditions on those early plantations were appalling, but this of course did not prevent the colonists, British to the bitter end, from religiously observing "tea time."

On steamy verandas overlooking large estates hacked out of the jungle, planters would place pith helmets and canes on the table before ritually drinking their tea in the tepid breeze of a punkah fanned by a servant. Tea was occasionally accompanied by spice buns, cakes and sandwiches.

Now the world's leading producer and number two exporter of tea (just after Ceylon), India is also a major tea-drinking country. Tea is drunk especially in the north, since southern Indians prefer coffee. Tiny tea stalls line the sidewalks of northern cities, where all day long *chayvalas* (tea sellers) serve customers seated on small benches. The carefully brewed *chai* is kept constantly hot in a sort of samovar, and a glass costs only a few rupees. It is usually served very strong, with lots of sugar and milk (often concentrated). Hurried customers often pour a little tea in the saucer to cool it before drinking. As a popular national beverage, tea is also drunk at home, in the city and in the smallest of villages. In the Punjab, to the north, tea is mixed with boiling milk and strong spices.

But anyone who has traveled through India, particularly in the suffocating, dehydrating heat of the monsoon season, has noted and appreciated the wonderful institution of serving tea in trains and stations. It is kept hot in large kettles and served in small clay cups that are shattered after use, thereby assuring travelers that no member of a

"Tea is the beverage of ceremonious peoples, and like the dense monsoon rains, it is both calming and stimulating, encouraging conversation and relaxation. . . . Ideas and traditions steep slowly in its steamy transparence." Pascal Bruckner, *Parias. Opposite*: A teapot heating on the burner, next to pepper and red chillies used in the spicy tea of northern India.

lower caste has drunk from the same vessel. In large stations—which in India are like small cities that throb with life day and night—the former "retiring rooms" have been transformed into inexpensive bedrooms. If you stay the night, a boy dressed in white will knock on the door at about six in the morning and announce in a loud voice: "Morning tea! Morning tea!" In this vast country with its changing landscapes, tea is associated with travel, long journeys during which season and climate vary from region to region. In the foothills of the Himalayas, tea braces voyagers against the cold, and its warmth favors human contact. "In my unbroken solitude," wrote P. Bruneton in *En solitaire dans l'Himalaya*, "I learned to take delight in the pleasure afforded by a cup of tea. When I would go in at dusk, the gentle warmth of tea filled me as night closed in around my eyrie. A simple cup of tea has often been the only spark needed to make an acquaintance, inaugurating a bond of friendship that could last a lifetime!"

"Here I am, as usual, comfortably installed in a first-class compartment. This is the sixth train I have taken since arriving in India. . . . If I board at night, an employee waits at the station to indicate the compartment reserved for me; at daybreak, barely have I opened my eyes when I am served *chota-khazri* (that is to say tea, a biscuit and a banana—a sort of appetizer before breakfast)." Ferdinand Goetel, *Voyage aux Indes*, 1937. *Above:* A hawker carries his utensils in the monsoon-flooded streets of Porbandar. *Opposite:* Serving tea on an Indian train sometimes resembles a highwire act more than room service, since the vestibule between the restaurant car and the first-class carriages is locked to prevent other passengers from importuning first-class travelers.

TO MEDITERRANEAN SHORES

Prior to the sixteenth-century discovery of maritime routes linking Europe to Asia, the taste for tea spread west very slowly, in the wake of caravans. Yet it probably reached Afghanistan, that hub of major trade routes (notably the famous silk route), at an early date, and to this day tea remains the country's national beverage. Afghans squat or sit cross-legged as they drink it at home or in *chaikhana* (local tea houses that are sometimes open-air affairs). Tradesmen, pilgrims, camel-drivers, and caravan travelers drink

In following caravan routes westward, the taste for tea evolved according to local customs. West Asian tea drinkers nevertheless share certain traits, notably the use of a samovar. This utensil was supposedly invented at the end of the eighteenth century by Ural metalsmiths, and has become inextricably linked to Russian tea, even though it is also used by Iranians and Afghans. *Above:* Women gathered around a samovar, Persia, nineteenth-century. *Opposite:* A tea dealer's stand in Afghanistan, late nineteenth century.

either green tea (*chai sabz*) for its thirst-quenching properties or black tea (*chai siyah*) when they want to warm themselves. They usually add lots of refined sugar, a symbol of wealth. Itinerant hawkers with samovars, stoves and comely teapots aligned on planks of wood also provide steaming tea to travelers along the roadside, occasionally sheltering under large tents of yak hide.

Chaikhana are exuberant, working-class places, and singers and musicians sometimes perform there. People come to chat, to discuss the latest village news, or to pass the time after work. Customers take off their shoes before sitting on mats or large, colorful rugs. Framed prints of Persian calligraphy line the walls, as do floral paintings that echo the patterns painted on the front of the house. Such images evoke springtime and the earth's fertility. Tea is served in round teapots of Risner porcelain imported from the former Soviet Union. But the recent war in Afghanistan, by halting Soviet imports, has led to a small industry in which Afghans carefully imitate the blue cover, red or blue band, and floral patterns invariably found on the original Russian models.

"Seated on a mat and drinking tea from porcelain bowls," wrote Ella Maillart in *La Voie cruelle*, "we admired the mountains toward which we were headed, then the amber fields surrounding the village. . . . Behind us, a row of round teapots gleamed softly in the recess of a shelf, while a boy fanned the charcoal under his samovar."

Caravans eventually brought tea to Mediterranean shores, reaching the Ottoman Empire and Egypt several centuries before it arrived in Western Europe. Contrary to popular belief, Turkey consumes less coffee than tea, which it grows and even exports. Pierre Loti discovered the pleasure of Turkish tea in sweltering Istanbul, where households keep tea constantly on the fire, adding hot water just before serving. This custom is so important to domestic life that mothers, before marrying off their sons, make sure that the future wife is fully conversant in *demilikaçay* (preparing tea). Another tradition still observed in Erzurum, near Iran, requires a host to continually refill a guest's glass until this latter places his teaspoon across the glass. This tradition has died out among most of Turkey's tea houses, or *çay-evi*, where tea is served in small, round glasses that fit snugly into the hand, warming it during the cold winter months.

Egypt is Africa's largest consumer of tea and the world's fifth biggest importer (after the United Kingdom, the Commonwealth of Independent States, the United States and Pakistan). Egyptians are truly passionate about tea. This passion weighs heavily on a steep balance of payments deficit, but the government must nevertheless subsidize tea in the same way that it subsidizes

"The souks open. The dark alcoves of the boutiques slowly appear. Tea merchants line up tray after tray. The delicate, chiseled designs of these trays glint in the light above the shoulders of agile carriers who bring them, bowl-laden, to the house. Yet I am struck by the number of consumers who go outside for nourishment; the desire to chat draws them out. I like these colorful drinking establishments. The owner oversees the huge copper kettles that boil and grumble. With a free hand, he wipes tiny glasses with a cloth that is used for everything." F. Balson, *De Kaboul au golfe Persique*, 1949. *Opposite:* A tea merchant's stall on the southern route through Afghanistan, between Kabul and Bamiyan, 1968.

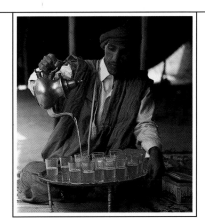

bread, sugar and oil, in order to maintain domestic peace. Tea is everywhere in Egypt—in homes and at the workplace, where it would be unthinkable to go through a day without sipping at least three or four glasses. This taste for tea goes back a long way (tea was drunk regularly at the sultan's court in the fifteenth century) and has reached every corner of the country. In September 1942, Rommel purchased the support of sheikhs at the Siwa oasis in the middle of the Libyan desert by offering them ten thousand Italian lire—and six pounds of tea. Egyptians generally drink a Dust-type tea from India or Ceylon, fairly strong and very sweet but without milk. In the numerous cafés in towns and villages, which often have no soft drinks to offer, customers are brought a glass of unsugared *chai* on a small pewter tray, accompanied by a glass of cold water, a small glass of sugar, a spoon and, on rare occasions, a third glass containing mint leaves. As in many other countries, tea is offered to every visitor to the home, whether stranger, friend or relation. In the houses of fellahs, it is drunk seated on mats placed on the ground. Tea and water—from the Nile—are heated together in a metal teapot placed on an oil stove. The tea is poured once into the glasses to warm them, then poured back into the teapot and finally into the glasses again.

Contrary to widespread belief, Islamic law does not forbid Muslims to drink black tea on the grounds that it is a fermented beverage. Most Islamic countries, including Egypt, Pakistan and Saudi Arabia, import and consume black tea from India or Ceylon. It would seem that the two main Islamic consumers of green tea—Morocco and Afghanistan—merely reflect local traditions and tastes. In Morocco, green tea is always used because it has become part and parcel of their traditional mint tea. This is nevertheless a recent tradition, since it dates back only to the mid-nineteenth century when British tea merchants, losing their Slavic market as a result of the Crimean War, sought new outlets. Moroccans welcomed tea with delight, for it cut the harshness of their usual brew of mint leaves alone. And they probably preferred green tea because it went well with the color and taste of mint. Moroccan tea is served in small glasses often painted with colorful designs, placed on a round tray of silver, silver-plate, or brass. Tea drinkers sit on long, fringed carpets. As in many Muslim countries, serving tea is a man's affair,

"Presently she returned, carrying an earthen pot of bright coals. While she was boiling the water and preparing the tea, Smaïl chatted with her . . . [and couldn't help but] marvel at the delicate movements of her nimble, henna-stained fingers as she tore the stalks of mint apart and stuffed them into the little teapot." Paul Bowles, *The Sheltering Sky*, 1949. *Above:* Mint tea on an oasis in southern Morocco. *Right:* A gilded, enameled teapot of Moorish design, displayed at the 1851 Universal Exhibition. *Opposite:* Tea in a private home in Fez, Morocco.

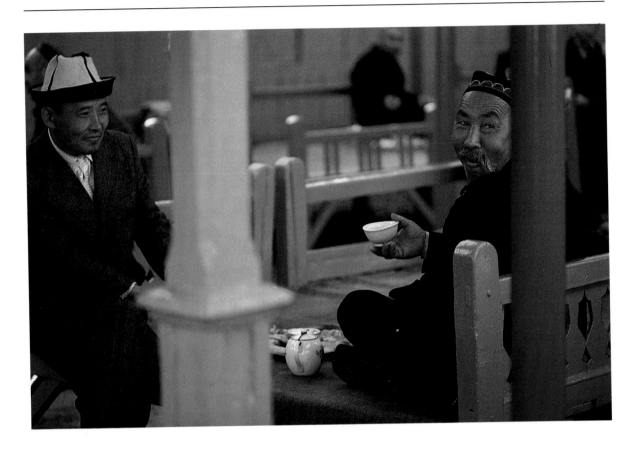

and is usually performed by the head of the family, thus symbolizing his role as husband, father, and host. The host uses two different teapots, pouring three successive glasses, from weakest to strongest, holding the teapot high above the glass to create a small head of foam on the tea. Mint tea is served at all hours of the day, accompanied by sweets. It is also drunk during meals, which are rather heavy and spicy, since it eases digestion. Indeed, Moroccans like to say that tea should be bitter as death, sweet as life, and as mellow as love.

THE LAND OF SAMOVARS

Imperial Russia discovered tea in 1638, when the ambassador Vassily Starkov deliv-

Tea time in a *chaikhana* in Kirghizia: "On summer evenings, the *chaikhana* is packed with people. Customers are seated both inside and on the outdoor terrace, its walls adorned with Kirghiz decorations and its carved roof held up by little columns. Roses scent the air. At this time of evening, the statue of Lenin stands out distinctly against the railing, his face turned toward the mountains." V. Vitkovich, *Allons voir la Kirghizie. Above:* A *chaikhana* in Kirghizia. *Preceding double page:* An Afghan *chaikhana.*

ered a Mongol prince's gift of one hundred and forty pounds of tea to Czar Mikhail Fedorovich. Although tea met with immediate success at court, it took two hundred years for it to become a common drink in the land of vodka. For until the eighteenth century, tea arrived from China by caravan, and was available only in a few cities. Moscow boasted the most connoisseurs, to the extent that Muscovites were long called "water drinkers."

Czar Alexander traveled with a large supply of tea when he visited Paris in 1814. He thereby introduced the French to "Russian tea" (which is, in fact, lightly smoked China tea). It quickly became popular in Parisian salons and society circles. In 1843, when Balzac was staying in Saint Petersburg (where he met Madame Hanska), the writer made a point of buying a great deal of what was then considered the finest tea available (not to be confused with the modern "Imperial Russian" blend of India, Ceylon and China teas scented with bergamot and other citrus flavors).

Tea was common throughout the Russian empire by the mid-nineteenth century, having been carried from market to market, even to the remotest of villages. The Russian word for "tip" comes from *na chai*, "for the tea." The spread of tea was accompanied by the invention of the samovar, which swiftly became a veritable institution imitated the world over. A samovar is a large recipient usually made of copper or bronze (though it also exists in other materials, from porcelain to gold), designed to keep water hot all day long with its charcoal-heated hot-air system. It is topped by a small teapot filled with *tscheinik*, a form of concentrated tea. A samovar also has a small spigot for adding water directly to cups or glasses. Tea-lovers leave the samovar bubbling—or "growling like a storm"—in their sitting room all day long. All great Russian authors, from Dostoevksi to Tolstoy and Gorky, have written about the warm intimacy created by a samovar. It can, however, sometimes disrupt an entire household, as Chekov amusingly described in *Uncle Vanya*: "At night, the professor read and wrote, and often, at around two o'clock in the morning, the bell would ring. . . . What's going on, children? Tea! Everyone had to be awakened to bring him the samovar. . . ."

These days, the Trans-Siberian railroad places a samovar at the disposal of travelers, who are allowed to

"I will provide a few details on what the Russians normally eat. Let's start with beverages. Rich Russians drink real [French] champagne . . . they drink the finest vintages of Bordeaux and Burgundy wines, to which they add various liqueurs produced all over the world. But since wine is very expensive in Russia, small merchants, employees and the common people drink tea during meals." Olympe Audouard, *Voyage aux pays des Boyards*, 1881. *Above:* Russian peasants around the family table, circa 1900.

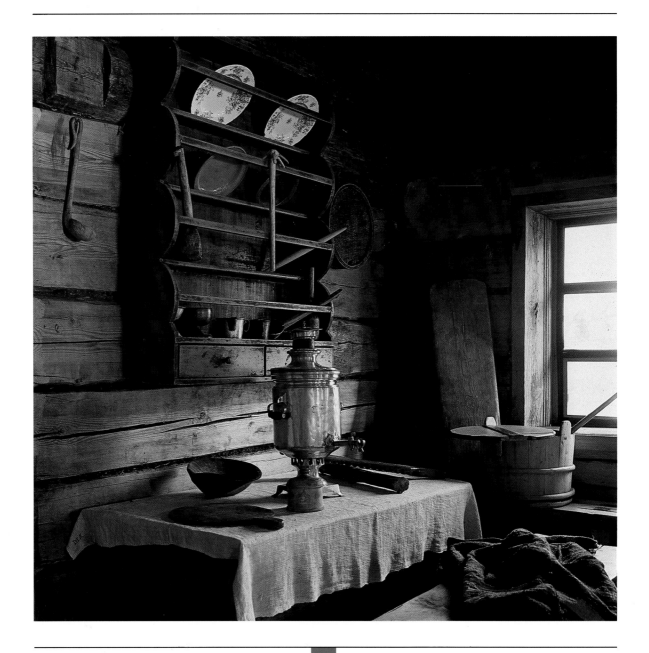

"He strongly insisted that Velchaninov . . . gulp down two or three cups of light tea. Without asking Velchaninov's permission, he ran to awaken Maura, and helped her to build a fire in the long-neglected kitchen, and boil some water in the samovar. . . . Twenty minutes later the tea was ready." Dostoevsky, "The Eternal Husband." *Above:* The traditional samovar in the kitchen of a nineteenth-century farmer's cabin. *Opposite:* A tea service that reportedly belonged to Czar Nicolas II.

bring their own tea. In every train station, a large kettle called a *kipjatok* provides hot water for a kopek. Russians drink both green and black tea, without milk, often in glasses with a metal handle. They eat a piece of unrefined sugar or a spoonful of fruit jam, which melts in the mouth when mixed with a sip of strong, bitter tea. "Ecstasy," wrote Pushkin, "is a glass full of tea and a piece of sugar in the mouth. . . . "

The former Soviet Union is now one of the main tea-producing regions in the world.

Yet domestic demand is still not met. And, the intensive, mechanized plantations in the newly independent republic of Georgia produce only a relatively poor quality of tea. Russia therefore imports tea from India and Ceylon for the urban middle classes as well as for privileged civil servants.

It is said that the finest harvests of "noble" tea placed on auction at the Colombo and Calcutta exchanges are almost always bought up by Russian importers, for whom tea is a priceless commodity.

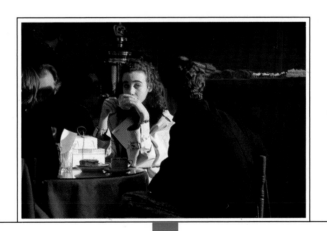

"The use of tea is so widespread in Russia that, at a single café-restaurant in Moscow which I will describe later, thirty-three pounds of tea is consumed on an average day, which makes nine hundred ninety pounds per month, or eleven thousand eight hundred eighty pounds per year!" Jacques Boucher de Perthes, *Voyage en Russie*, 1859. *Above:* Taking tea at Margarita's, a famous café in a Moscow park that has become the favorite haunt of Moscow youth. *Opposite, top:* A collection of nineteenth-century samovars in a country home near Moscow. *Opposite, bottom:* An early twentieth-century samovar in brass.

TEA AT GOETHE'S

Tea arrived in Germany by way of Holland, around 1640. It was long considered a medicinal plant and was used mostly by women, who would purchase it at the fashionable herbalist shops that were forerunners to today's pharmacies. But tea had become a part of everyday life by the end of the eighteenth century—in 1772, sixty types of tea were available on the German market, imported from China by the Royal Tea Company (founded 1752) via the ports of Hamburg and Bremen. It could even be taken in one of the magnificent gold- or silver-decorated china tea services produced by porcelain works in Meissen, Bayreuth and Ansbach.

It was around this time that Germans replaced their morning bowl of soup with tea. Soon they were drinking three or four cups a day. In the mid-nineteenth century, Germans adopted the English craze for "punch," a mixture of rum, brandy, sugar, lemon and tea, even though purists considered it a sacrilege to smother tea with alcohol. A little later, consumers acquired a taste for black teas, and by 1880 twenty percent of German imports came from India and Ceylon.

Tea became an indispensable element of high-society salons and artistic circles during the nineteenth century. The way in which it was served was sometimes even interpreted in amorous terms—a bit of froth on the surface of the liquid could represent the promise of a

It was at Meissen in Germany that the secret of how to manufacture china porcelain was finally discovered in 1709. The first tea services made in Europe were based on Chinese models. As in China, cups had no handles. Saucers were deep, without ridges, like a shallow bowl—and the cooling tea was sometimes drunk directly from it. *Above:* A painting by Jacob Denner, 1737, titled *Balthasar Denner and Family*. On the table is a tea urn instead of a Chinese-style teapot. *Opposite:* A portrait by Johann Heinrich Tischbein of his fiancée, painted in 1756. Here, the urn in the foreground contained hot water for tea.

love letter, or even a kiss. "They were seated around a table, drinking tea and talking of love," wrote the poet Heinrich Heine. Goethe believed a tea party was the perfect way to receive friends. In October 1823, his secretary, Eckermann, noted in what was to become the *Interviews* that "this evening I was invited to tea at Goethe's. I greatly enjoyed the company, very natural and casual; some were seated, others were standing, we joked and laughed. Goethe would go from one to the other and he seemed to take greater pleasure in letting his friends talk and listening to them, than in saying something himself. Frau Goethe entered several times, to hug and kiss him." Goethe, in fact, had just married his mistress, Christiane Vulpius, mother of his illegitimate son August. The highly proper ladies of the Weimar Society hesitated to receive her. It was Fraulein Göchlausen who finally made a decision: "If Goethe gave her his name, we can at least give her a cup of tea!"

Heinrich Heine wrote his famous poem on tea at one of Berlin's literary and artistic gathering spots, the Stehelysh tea and pastry shop. Painters, writers, actors and diplomats would meet there over a cup of tea, in the company of Rahel Varnhagen (Goethe's "darling child") and Henriette Herz (said to be the most beautiful woman in Berlin). The novelist Theodore Fontane was another regular, and Prince Ludwig-Ferdinand could be seen there on occasion with the charming Pauline Wiesel.

During the late nineteenth century—a period marked by an interest in Japanese art and by *Jugendstil*, the German Art Nouveau movement—tea was favored over coffee by the sensitive, sentimental younger generation,

The fashion for things Chinese, which had gripped all of Europe by the seventeenth century, also had an effect on landscape art. Pinnacled temples and pagodas sprang up in parks and gardens, as did tea houses. European tea houses were only distantly related to the Chinese original, but the idea was exotic and China tea was consumed there. *Above:* One of the finest existing examples of these tea houses can be seen in the gardens of the Sans Soucis château in Potsdam. It was built in the eighteenth century by Frederick II of Prussia. *Opposite:* The decoration and sculptures adorning the façade of this delightful pavilion offer a whimsical view of the Orient. *Left:* A gilded porcelain teapot manufactured in Meissen, circa 1725.

who found it more in keeping with the mildly melancholic mood of the day. In the 1920s, on the other hand, German youth was enthusiastic about revolutionary Russia, and it drank "Russian tea" during all-night discussions on how to change the world. Several years later, Germany acquired the European penchant for "tea dances." Grand hotels transformed their bars into ballrooms where all generations would mix on the dance floor between cups of tea. Slang expressions from those years include "let the tea steep" (meaning "forget it") and "tea kettle" (to describe "a clod").

Today it is Hamburg merchants—dynamic businessmen and heirs to a long tradition of trading in tea—who control a large part of the international tea market, surpassing even London in terms of quality. The average German now drinks two or three times as much tea as a Frenchman, and some Germans—notably those in East Friesland near the Dutch border—even consume as much as the English. Frisians, in fact, were the first Germans to adopt tea, and fishermen along the coast used to drink a strong blend of Assam and Java tea mixed with rum. Even if this lusty cocktail is no longer popular, residents of East Friesland still like to drink tea during meals and throughout the day. A little fresh cream is sometimes added to the brew. In summer, tea is drunk iced, to the great delight of children.

"When [von Aschenbach] entered the breakfast-room it was empty. Guests came in while he sat waiting for his order to be filled. As he sipped his tea he saw the Polish girls enter with their governess, chaste and morning-fresh, with sleep-reddened eyelids." Thomas Mann, *Death in Venice*, 1911. *Above:* A book of musical scores for tea dances, 1935. *Opposite, top:* A lithograph by Koch entitled *The Bachelor's Visit*, 1880. *Opposite, bottom:* A 1902 print captioned, "At tea time, women should be taken for what they are." Based on a watercolor by Oscar Bluhm.

Scenes of "Dutch tea" showing how highly the Dutch valued tea kettles (felt in other European countries to be inelegant and impractical). *Above:* A handsome tea salon, a room specially set aside for this purpose in seventeenth-century Dutch homes, and a depiction of a tea-drinker on Delft faïence. *Opposite:* In the eighteenth century, when Nicolas Muys executed this painting, the Dutch had become accustomed to drinking large quantities of tea—Montesquieu wrote in his *Voyage en Hollande* that he was amazed to see a mistress of the house drink thirty cups at a single sitting!

TEA AND SCONES

Tea is more than just a tradition for the English—it is a way of life. The average Briton drinks six cups of tea per day. In the seventeenth and eighteenth centuries, the advent of tea—like the spread of industry—represented a revolution. As a sign of good taste and a mark of conviviality, it swiftly became an integral part of British society at all levels, significantly changing people's daily life insofar as the day became organized around "tea time." Taking tea was both a working-class and aristocratic affair, becoming highly codified and extremely refined in sophisticated homes. Probably nowhere else in the world has a beverage so pleasantly governed the day of an entire nation.

Handles on cups did not become popular until the end of the eighteenth century. The idea of a handle was supposedly borrowed from the mugs in which the English drank hot wine and beer. By freeing themselves from the Chinese model, European tea services could then evolve toward a wide variety of forms. British factories strove to be ingenious, even producing "mustache cups" with an inner ridge designed to keep elegant mustaches dry. *Above:* Taking tea in England, circa 1740. *Opposite: A Gentleman at Breakfast*, circa 1775, attributed to Henry Walton.

It is perhaps best symbolized by the "early morning cuppa" sipped in bed on awakening, prior to washing and dressing. Each day is thus inaugurated under the sign of tea. As Cecil Roth recounted, "I was recently the guest of Baron Alfred de Rothschild in his Seamore Place palace. Early in the morning, a liveried servant entered my room pushing a huge table on wheels. He asked, 'Would you like tea or a peach, sir?' I chose tea, which immediately provoked another question. 'China, India, or Ceylon, sir?' When I asked for India tea, he enquired, 'With lemon, cream, or milk, sir?' I opted for milk, but he wanted to know which breed of cow I preferred: 'Jersey, Hereford or Sorthorn, sir?' Never had I drunk such a good cup of tea." The "early morning cuppa" is obviously to be followed by an English breakfast of porridge, fish, scrambled or fried eggs and bacon, all washed down by more tea. Such a breakfast is a far cry from the sugary "continental breakfast" eaten in Europe's Latin countries.

The first public sale of tea in England took place in 1657, during Cromwell's stewardship. Trader Thomas Garraway vaunted the drink's numerous medicinal properties. It was swiftly adopted by the cream of London

"Five o'clock tea," served on a low table laid with small sandwiches and light pastries, is quite distinct from "high tea," a solid working-class meal eaten at the family table and constituting the main repast of the day for laborers back from field or factory. *Above:* A photograph taken by William Henry Fox Talbot in 1840, *The Breakfast Table.* This is the first photograph taken of an English tea service. *Opposite:* An 1874 painting titled *Reading the News* by James Tissot, a French artist who lived in London and often included a tea table in his compositions.

society. Women would often withdraw to a sitting room after dinner to drink tea, while the men remained at the table with their port. Thanks to the success of coffee houses, where tea could be procured, the lower classes also had relatively early access to the beverage. In 1660, Samuel Pepys wrote in his diary: "I did send for a cup of tee (a China drinke) of which I had never drank before." The spectacular rise of tea in England was linked to the success of coffee houses, the first of which opened in London in 1652. Fifty years later the capital boasted no fewer than five hundred coffee houses. These establishments became the unrivaled social centers of English life in the seventeenth and eighteenth centuries, for here customers could drink tea, coffee, brandy or rum, and sample a range of delicacies, all the while perusing British and continental newspapers or casually chatting. Apparently, it was here that the European version of tipping was

Despite the unpredictability of English weather, drinking tea outdoors has always been considered an ideal way to pass the time. During the warmer months, some events are intimately bound up with the practice of taking tea on the lawn. Buckingham Palace garden parties, Henley regattas, cricket matches and village festivals all provide an opportunity to sample tea, sandwiches and cakes under large tents specially erected for the occasion. *Above:* Ladies in a garden, Loughton, 1908. *Opposite:* Taking tea on the lawn, photographed by Mortimer around 1900.

born—customers could toss a coin into a box marked T.I.P. ("To Insure Promptness").

In 1706, Thomas Twining, then a young salesman for a London tea merchant, founded "Tom's Coffee House," the first such establishment to specialize in tea. He thus launched what was to become one of the most famous tea rooms in the world. As recounted above, Twining opened a retail shop, The Golden Lyon, eleven years later. This was where women, who were not admitted to coffee houses, could buy and drink their tea. Throughout the eighteenth century, the consumption of tea rose sharply. Fifteen times as much tea was drunk at the close of the century as at the outset. In the final fifteen years alone, consumption doubled as the habit of drinking tea filtered down from the

Like their parents, the children of good Edwardian families were highly attached to the ritual of taking tea, associated as it was with sweets and the security of nursery life. J. M. Barrie's story *Peter Pan* demonstrates that budding Britons prefer tea time to the marvelous universe of an enchanted isle: "'Do you want an adventure now,' Peter said casually to John, 'or would you like to have your tea first?' Wendy said, 'Tea first,' quickly." J. M. Barrie, *Peter Pan*, 1904. *Above: A Cheerful Giver*, by Fred Morgan, circa 1900.

aristocracy to the middle and lower classes. The swift spread of tea was linked to a sharp cut in the tea tax ordained by Pitt in 1783, an attempt to undermine an increasingly well-organized black market that profited from a commerce employing over forty thousand people and three hundred ships.

The craze for tea during the latter half of the century had already led to the creation of "tea gardens." England revived the art of landscape gardening by abandoning French formalism to celebrate nature in all its romantic forms. Londoners from all walks of life could enjoy refined gardens at Ranelagh, Marylebone, and Vauxhall. There, in a Gainsborough-like setting where the baroque competed with the classical, strollers could sit on a patch of grass or around a table, not far from a rococo temple or the remnant of a column. They might hear the strains of an orchestra as they sipped a cup of tea, accompanied by bread, butter, or cake, or even a tasty combination of a morsel between two slices of bread, recently invented by the clever Lord John Sandwich.

It was during the Victorian era that "lunch"—a midday meal enabling men

to get together at the club and women to meet at home—took on greater importance. Slowly, eating times and habits changed. Dinner took place at seven or eight o'clock instead of five or six, so that the supper normally eaten at ten at night became superfluous. It was in 1840 that Anna, seventh duchess of Bedford, invented "afternoon tea" to be taken at home at four o'clock (the appointed hour becoming five o'clock early in the twentieth century). This was a way to quell the inevitable hunger pangs between lunch and dinner, and became so popular among affluent classes that it not only provoked the decline of tea gardens but became one of the mainstays of the British way of life.

Afternoon tea was taken before a fire in the drawing room in winter, but might be enjoyed in the shade of a tree in the garden during summer. It represented an agreeable if strictly regulated marriage of good taste, refinement and sociability. One dressed comfortably yet elegantly, and full, light "tea gowns" (simpler and less tightly cinched at the waist than ordinary gowns) were created in the 1880s. A fine tablecloth and china or silver tea service were also required;

"Ten minutes later, they were sitting downstairs in the comfortable kitchen being introduced to Curtis, a rather gruff-looking, grey-haired old man, and being regaled with strong tea, bread and butter, Devonshire cream and hard-boiled eggs. While they ate and drank they listened. Within half an hour they knew everything there was to be known about the inhabitants of the small community." Agatha Christie, *The Sittaford Mystery*, 1931. *Above:* A 1930 Empire Marketing Board poster titled *And We'll All Have Tea.*

this would include a teapot, milk pitcher, sugar bowl, several tightly sealed tea caddies, twelve cups, saucers, plates and caddy spoons. Finally, and above all, the mistress of the house had to be expert in preparing the tea and the light meal that went with it. Naturally, it was in the best of taste to have everything served by a domestic or, even better, by the young lady of the house who could thereby demonstrate the savoir-faire and refinement needed to enter society. She must, for instance, pour milk into the cup prior to pouring the tea; the tea itself must come from India or Ceylon, which produced the only two types of tea considered proper.

Right from the start, the buffet meal accompanying afternoon tea was systematized once and for all. Guests were entitled to small cucumber, tomato, egg or watercress sandwiches, or toast with cinnamon, almond biscuits, scones, jam (usually strawberry), various pound and sponge cakes. Soon "cream teas" became fashionable, the tea being accompanied by freshly clotted cream. Children, who were served tea in the nursery in the Victorian and Edwardian periods, were notably allowed to have sandwiches made with sardines, chocolate or bananas, or perhaps muffins

and crumpets with jellies and jams, as well as all sorts of sweet or savory cakes. Naturally enough, little girls would sit their dolls around a miniature tea service.

In the countryside, afternoon tea was taken on returning from the fields, and therefore became the main meal of the day. In many cottages and farms, where hospitality was the rule, it was not unusual to see a sign over the doorway inviting travelers or even vagabonds to come in for a cup of tea with scones, buns or home-made bacon pie.

Local traditions sprang up in all corners of the kingdom, from clotted cream in Devon, to eggs and conserves in the west country, to apple cake in Dorset. In Cornwall, the use of sugar was banned the day Methodist preacher John Wesley recommended boycotting it as a way of discouraging slavery in the West Indies.

In "elegant and polite" country homes, tea would be taken either in a small drawing room or the veranda or garden arbor, depending on the season. Tea might be drunk from Stafford porcelain during endless bridge parties, or between two innings of cricket, sets of tennis, or games of croquet. Iced tea and sandwiches

Three British versions of tea time. *Above:* The spare Welsh style. *Opposite, top:* A Rene Mackintosh interior for the recently restored Glasgow tea rooms founded by Miss Cranston, the temperance crusader. *Opposite, bottom:* A 1925 tea room that continues to fulfill Londoners' rural yearnings—this "Tea House at College Farm" is still located on a small farm in north London.

soon became a popular treat during the hottest days of summer.

Among the middle and lower urban classes, four o'clock tea also became more than a simple break, evolving into a substantial meal of sandwiches made of meat, fish, pâté or cheese. If they were unable to take tea at home, modest Londoners would flock to the tea houses that flourished in the wake of the amazing success of A.B.C. tea rooms.

The Aerated Bread Company had launched its tea rooms in 1864. Women were allowed to enter unaccompanied, and such tea houses soon took over from the tea gardens.

Queen Victoria could hardly find fault with this, for she officially instituted tea time at Buckingham Palace. As an adolescent, Victoria had been obliged to bend to the somewhat fanatical will of her governess, the duchess of Northumberland, who was

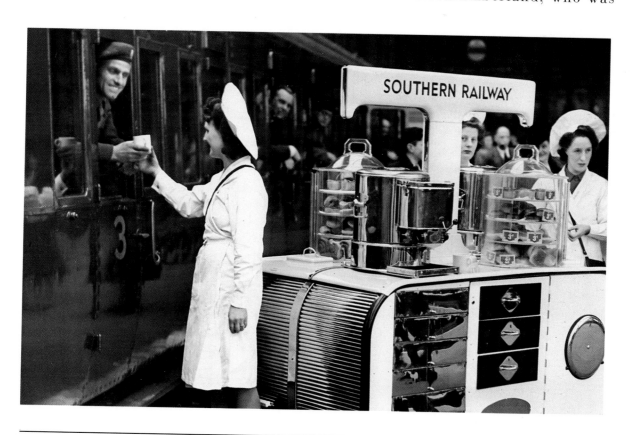

By the nineteenth century, Britons considered tea an essential element of daily well-being, and subsequently linked it to the social health of the country. *Above:* In 1946, when the government promised that the standard of living would improve, railway travelers saw ultra-modern tea trolleys appear in train stations. *Opposite:* In a Welsh county where the unemployment rate hit 90 percent in some towns in 1935, an event was organized to offer tea to disadvantaged children, not unlike the "tea moralities" of the Victorian era.

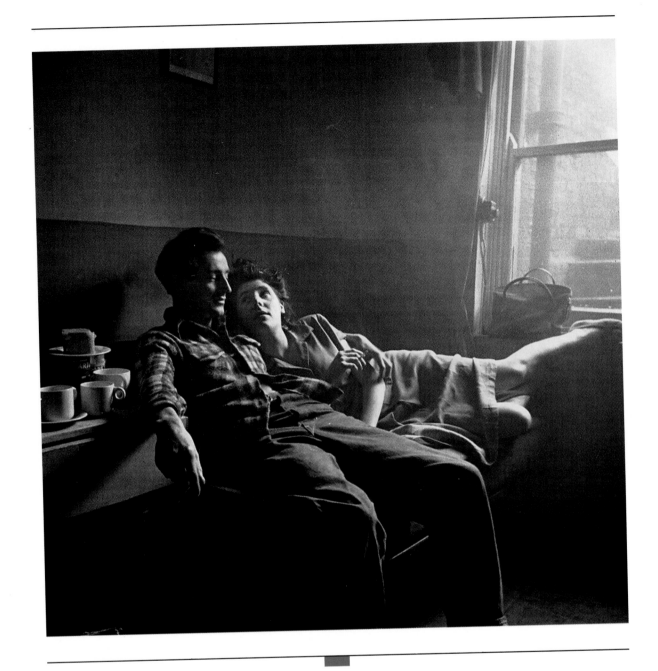

"'What tea do you drink?' asked Wyatt. 'I don't know anything about tea. Told Abdul to get some. Thought that girl might like to come in to tea one day. Darned pretty girl. Must do something for her. She must be bored to death in a place like this. . . .'" Agatha Christie, *The Sittaford Mystery*, 1931. *Above:* London, 1949. *Opposite:* Afternoon tea in Torquay, a tourist stop in southern England, 1954.

convinced of the diabolical effects of two highly fashionable activities—reading *The Times* and drinking tea. Victoria respectfully obeyed until 1838, the year of her coronation. Directly after the ceremony, the young queen took a deep breath, then asked for the latest *Times* and a cup of tea. Liveried servants carried out her orders instantly. "Now I know that I truly reign," she is reported to have said. Tea remained one of the queen's two favorite beverages. The other was whisky.

Throughout her sixty-four-year reign, Victoria supported "Tea Moralities," tea parties organized by charitable societies on behalf of underprivileged groups such as the unemployed, the homeless, and prostitutes. A comforting cup of tea, offered with the approval of God and queen, was also supposed to encourage a new habit among popula-

tions ravaged by alcoholism. The wretchedness of London's poor was evoked by Charles Dickens with humor and tenderness in his description of the melancholy cheer of Christmas so dear to the English. "The blended scents of tea and coffee were so grateful to the nose," he wrote in *A Christmas Carol*, " . . . the raisins were so plentiful and rare, the almonds so extremely white . . . the candied fruits so caked and spotted with molten sugar as to make the coldest lookers-on feel faint. . . . " Another tradition sprang up as the industrial revolution spread: the tea break, a mid-morning and mid-afternoon pause enabling staff and workers to drink a cup of tea and have a snack. But it was not until unions fought for the right to a tea break around 1820 that this practice, so energetically resisted by employers in the

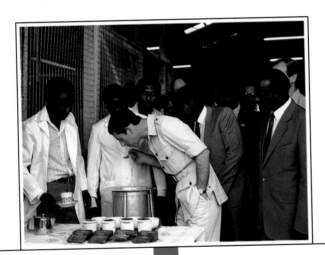

Above: The prince of Wales sampling Cameroon tea. *Opposite:* A 1950 painting by Sir James Gunn showing the royal family of England taking tea at Windsor Castle. Every afternoon, King George VI, his wife Elizabeth and the two young princesses assembled around a cup of tea accompanied by watercress sandwiches, kirsch-flavored cake or coffee éclairs. Today, the current monarch, Elizabeth II, concludes all business and returns to her apartments at five o'clock sharp—tea time. The tea comes from Twinings, the china from Worcester, and the queen uses these precious moments to meet with her children or look after her pet corgis.

name of productivity, became the rule.

Like many other tea-related traditions, this twice-daily break is on the decline in Britain. Office hours, new technology, the mass arrival of women in the labor force and new dietary concerns have considerably altered eating and drinking habits. Automatic drink dispensers have transformed the break into a swizzling of some wretched concoction—perched on the corner of the desk—at no particular time of day. The tradition of "high tea," a veritable evening meal composed of cold meat, scrambled eggs and bacon, salad, cakes and fruit, as well as the ubiquitous cup of tea, is now observed only in the rural north of England and in Scotland.

In London, the most delectable and refined afternoon tea is served in the tea rooms of grand hotels. Take, for example, the menu proposed by Brown's Hotel for five o'clock tea: in addition to an excellent selection of teas (including their own blend and a green tea), the menu lists a variety of small sandwiches, toast and jam, scones and clotted cream, cakes and the chef's own pastries. *Above:* Tea in a suite at Claridge's. *Opposite:* Brown's tea service, with afternoon tea menus from the Waldorf, the Ritz, the Savoy and Brown's, on a sheet featuring designs of eighteenth-century Minton china.

Should one want to indulge in the full ritual of "afternoon tea," this is generally done in the salon of one of the grand hotels, unless one is lucky enough to be invited to tea by the queen or a member of the gentry. The ceremony duly takes place every day at the Waldorf, the Ritz, the Savoy and Brown's. In the Palm Court at the Ritz, for instance, with its plush setting that combines Louis XVI design with Art Deco, carefully muted lighting gives customers the pleasant impression of being cut off from the world, far from the bustle of Piccadilly. The chimerical atmosphere is enhanced by palm trees and a fountain adorned with mermaids and tritons contemplated by a languid nymph. An impeccably trained staff sets china tea services on marble tables, serving Darjeeling or Earl Grey to a clientele that dresses for the occasion. Customers may partake of time-honored varieties of finger sandwiches pre-pared by a famous "sandwich chef." The cucumber, cream cheese and smoked salmon sandwiches are made with dark bread, whereas the smoked ham, egg salad and watercress and cheddar sandwiches are served on white. Then come deliciously fresh scones, accompanied by cream and strawberry jam, and finally cakes and petits fours.

Even if the nature and ritual of "afternoon tea" have been considerably simplified in recent years, it remains a special and often indispensable part of the day for the British. What Paul Morand wrote in *Le Nouveau Londres* still applies to modern England. "To say, at about five o'clock, 'I haven't yet had tea,' can upset an entire household; complete strangers practically feel obliged to offer you 'a nice cup of tea'—from Ceylon, naturally, even though ever since the island gained its independence tea is also grown in Argentina and the Azores."

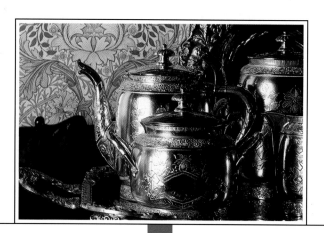

"The cup of tea on arrival at a country house is a thing which, as a rule, I particularly enjoy. I like the crackling logs, the shaded lights, the scent of buttered toast, the general atmosphere of leisured cosiness." P. G. Wodehouse, *The Code of the Woosters. Above:* A Scottish silver tea service. *Opposite:* In a traditional Scottish manor, the table is set for afternoon tea.

FROM THE BOSTON TEA PARTY TO INSTANT TEA

As might be expected, English immigrants to America took "tea time" with them. Tea was introduced into North America as early as the seventeenth century by the Dutch, and its consumption became more widespread in the following century, particularly among the upper classes who so enjoyed tea parties. Such parties, with their silver teapots and porcelain tea services, became the symbol of social success, occasions at which the elite families of Philadelphia and Boston would meet. Soon, however, tea was also drunk in less affluent circles, becoming a universal sign of good manners and hospitality. In New York, the Chatham Street pump was thought to provide the best water for tea. "Tea-water men" hawked it loudly through the streets of the city. In the early eighteenth century, Puritans drank bitter tea with butter and salt, whereas most New Englanders preferred green China tea scented with saffron, iris root or gardenia petals. Such habits waned over the decades, but tea continued to be a popular beverage. By the end of the eighteenth century, a third of the colonies' population drank it twice a day.

Tea was thus the third-ranking colonial import during the 1760s, behind textiles and manufactured goods. When England found itself financially strapped by the French and Indian War, it levied a heavy tax on tea. Throughout the colonies, the tea tax provoked violent patriotic reaction and calls for

Two years after the Boston Tea Party, it was a silversmith by the name of Paul Revere (known for his silver teapots) who determined the outcome of the first battle between the English and the Americans at Lexington. On the night of 18 April 1775, Revere climbed the stairs of the highest steeple in Boston, carrying two lanterns to signal the American patriots of the arrival of British troops—"one if by land, two if by sea." From that point onward, Revere changed the design of his teapots, abandoning his rococo style to invent a "patriotic teapot." Its sober, pure, neoclassic design symbolized democratic values. *Opposite:* Portrait of Paul Revere by John Singleton Copley. *Above:* A painting by Johann Eckstein (1736-1817) titled *The Samuels Family*.

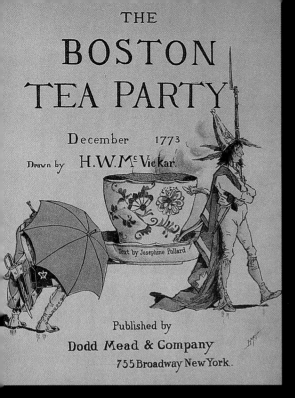

THE
BOSTON
TEA PARTY

December 1773

Drawn by H.W. Mc Vickar.

Text by Josephine Pollard.

Published by

Dodd Mead & Company

755 Broadway New York.

AND A MEETING WAS HELD, WHERE THE PROCLAMATION
WAS READ, THAT HAD CAUSED ALL THIS PERTURBATION.

A SCORE OR MORE MEN ON A NIGHT IN DECEMBER,
WENT FORTH TO A DEED THE WORLD WOULD REMEMBER.

HE WAS READY TO BURST WITH RAGE NO DOUBT,
WHEN THE CLERK IN A LOUD VOICE READ ABOUT

a boycott. An alarmed East India Company had the tax lowered, but this was not enough to cool tempers. On 16 December 1773, patriots from Saint Andrew's masonic lodge in Boston dressed up as Mohawk Indians and boarded three of the company's ships. They threw three hundred and forty chests of tea into the harbor. The incident became ironically known as the "Boston Tea Party," and unleashed English reprisals. But such action merely triggered other tea parties, ultimately leading to the battle of Bunker Hill and the Declaration of Independence in 1776. Tea had indeed started a revolution.

In the late eighteenth century, the young American merchant fleet entered the tea trade by going straight to the source—China. Imports of tea then rose spectacularly, going from six hundred tons in 1790 to ten times that amount in 1825. Numerous New England fortunes were built on this trade, money that was subsequently invested in local textile mills. In the face of a wave of new immigrants from Europe and Asia, the affluent classes in New England clung to the time-honored English traditions. Tea, along with hunting, became a social ritual designed to indicate membership in a privileged group. At the same time, tea became highly prized by the grand southern planters, and during the American civil war "blockade runners" supplied plantations with tea worth its weight in gold.

Oliver Wendell Holmes (1809-1894) wrote in his *Ballad of the Boston Tea Party:*

The waters in the rebel bay
Have kept the tea-leaf savor;
Our old North-Enders in their spray
Still taste a Hyson flavor;

And freedom's teacup still o'erflows
With ever-fresh libations,
To cheat of slumber all her foes
And cheer the wakening nations!

Above and opposite: Excerpts from a commemorative album published in New York in 1882. *Below:* Stamps issued for the bicentenary of the Boston Tea Party.

In the early twentieth century, a New York tea merchant named Thomas Sullivan had the bright idea of manufacturing tiny bags of silk containing a single dose of tea. This invention met with immediate and long-lasting success, radically changing the art of preparing tea and leading, alas, to the production of poor-quality tea better suited to being crushed and packed in bags. At roughly the same time, in 1904, tea dealer Richard Blechynden went to the Saint Louis World's Fair to introduce Americans to black tea from India, which until then was an unknown commodity. But the summer weather was sweltering, and visitors were not inclined to rush to Blechynden's stand to drink a hot cup of tea. Though thirsty, Blechynden himself shrank from the idea. So he put two ice cubes in a glass and poured the tea over them. Iced tea was born. Many fair-goers refreshed themselves with the new drink, and iced tea soon spread throughout the southern states.

Americans still drink a great deal of iced tea, often with lemon and sugar, sometimes with a dash of rum. This has led to a booming trade in "instant tea," a freeze-dried powder to be dissolved in cold water. Needless to say, tea connoisseurs do not think much of the product. Americans increasingly drink ready-made tea sold in cans, thereby significantly altering "tea consciousness" in their country. Without such initiatives, however, the United States (a country that consumes five times as much coffee as tea-based beverages) would certainly not be the world's third-largest importer of tea.

"Make up a good fire in the library, please, and bring the tea up . . . after rearranging her dark hair before the mirror, [she] carefully dressed herself in a loose garment of velvet and lace which lay awaiting her on the sofa. . . . She had been one of the first women in New York to have tea every afternoon at five o'clock, and to put off her walking-dress for a tea-gown." Edith Wharton, *New Year's Day*, 1923. *Above:* American advertising image. *Opposite: Tea Leaves*, a 1909 painting by the American artist W. Paxton depicting the practice of attempting to read the future in tea leaves. *Preceding double page:* Tea time in New England, circa 1900.

FRENCH SAVOIR-FAIRE

By the end of the 1630s, tea was already being appreciated in several small Parisian social circles, having been introduced at court by Cardinal Mazarin, who took it for his gout. As in most other countries, therefore, tea won its first French converts due to its medicinal properties. In the second half of the seventeenth century, scholarly books abounded in which tea's often controversial merits were vaunted and compared to those of other new products such as coffee and chocolate. In the France of that time, knowledge of both medicine and tea were far from having reached the degree of sophistication found in China, and as late as 1692 a certain François Massialot advocated "smoking tea like tobacco, after having lightly dampened the leaves with a dew-like sprinkling of brandy; also, the sediment or ashes remaining in the bowl of the pipe is marvelous for whitening the teeth."

Things exotic were highly fashionable. So when the *Amphitrite*, the first French ship to return from China, unloaded its costly cargo in 1700, moneyed *précieuses* (ostentatiously stylish women) were able to procure tea as well as silks, screens, lacquers, porcelain, rhubarb, and camphor. The beverage made from the Chinese plant became more widespread in high society during the reign of Louis XIV, when it was considered a pleasant and convivial refreshment beneficial even to the healthy. But Paris salons remained divided between advocates and detractors, and tea became an excellent subject of

The habit of putting milk in tea reportedly started in France. Madame de Sévigné described how Madame de la Sablière launched the fashion: "Madame de la Sablière took her tea with milk, as she told me the other day, because it was to her taste." In fact, there was a practical reason for this custom—pouring a little cold milk in the cup prevented the scalding tea from cracking fragile porcelain from China. This is apparently behind the English insistence on "M.I.F." ("milk in first"). *Above: Woman Taking Tea,* by J. B. S. Chardin. *Opposite: Toilette,* by François Boucher, 1742. *Preceding double page: English Tea in Paris, at the Prince de Conti's Court,* with the young Mozart at the harpsichord, by Olivier Barthelemy, 1766.

Unlike the British, the French have never considered tea, which is a stimulant, suitable for children. In spite of these reservations, however, generations of little girls have received miniature tea services as a gift. "Your Aunt D'Aubert instructed me to give you this little tea set as a gift from her. . . . The delighted Sophie took the tray with its six cups, teapot, silver sugar bowl and creamer." Comtesse de Ségur, *Les Malheurs de Sophie. Above: Francisque Sarcex at the Home of Adolphe Brisson's Daughter*, by M. A. Baschet. *Opposite: The Cup of Tea*, by M. A. Baschet, 1896. In 1925 Maurice Ravel directed a French child to drink tea on stage, in *L'Enfant et les sortilèges*.

conversation. The marquise de Sévigné, a great supporter of tea, witnessed some serious tea-drinking: "Saw the princesse de Tarente . . . who takes twelve cups of tea every day . . . which, she says, cures all her ills. She assured me that Monsieur le Landgrave drank forty cups every morning. 'But Madame, perhaps it is really only thirty or so.' 'No, forty. He was dying, and it brought him back to life before our eyes.'" Nicolas Audiger, author of *La Maison Réglée* (The Well-Ordered Household), added that tea "is normally taken in the morning to awaken the mind and stimulate the appetite." This opinion, however, was not completely shared by a vivacious princess of the Palatinate. "Tea is not as necessary for Protestant ministers as for Catholic priests who cannot marry," she claimed, "because it makes one chaste."

In France, tea remained rarer and much more expensive than coffee for a long time. Moreover, it was associated with costly utensils of porcelain and silver, unlike coffee which was soon being hawked in the streets and offered in the new, popular establishments known as cafés. By 1715, Paris boasted nearly three hundred of them. Tea was therefore the prerogative of wealthy families, a sign of utmost distinction, and an opportunity for the finest silversmiths and potters from the Vincennes and Sèvres factories to exercise their talent. Tea was perhaps too heavily marked by its Parisian, aristocratic beginnings to become a truly popular beverage in France. It was not until the nineteenth century that the new bourgeoisie and provincial gentry dared taste it, albeit gingerly. In *Illusions Perdues*, the tea-loving Balzac described a woman from Angoulême who "loudly informed the entire province of an evening

In France, tea rooms—as distinct from cafés—were for a long time the only public place that women could frequent without endangering their reputations. In her *Mémoires d'une jeune fille rangée*, Simone de Beauvoir recalled how college youths from good families would take her to tea in the back rooms of bakery shops, rather than in the tea salons that were too expensive for students. "They did not frequent cafés, and in any case would never have taken girls there." *Above:* Teapots in the Grand Hôtel de Cabourg. *Opposite:* The Fauchon tea rooms in Paris in 1910, and packets of tea formerly used by Mariage Frères tea dealers.

party of ice cream, cake and tea, a great innovation in a city where tea was still sold at apothecaries as a remedy for indigestion." During this very period, the British were drinking tea six times a day, from Buckingham Palace to the Liverpool slums.

By the end of the nineteenth century, however, thanks to "tea salons" and "tea dances," the beverage had become fairly common in sophisticated circles. Seaside resorts, with their casinos, flower-studded verandas and grand hotels such as the Hôtel du Palais in Biarritz and the Grand Hôtel in Cabourg, provided the perfect occasion to take tea with Proustian languor, letting conversation drift along pleasantly. The Bois de Boulogne near Paris also offered arbor-shaded tables at the Bagatelle, to which one could be conspicuously driven by landau.

France can at least pride itself on having invented the *salon de thé*, or fancy tea room so rare in an England where fine tea can now be had only in a grand hotel. Such salons have flourished in Paris since the early twentieth century, like the establishment founded in 1903 by Antoine Rumpelmeyer, a confectioner of Viennese origin; now known as Angelina, the tea room is still popular today. Faithful to the traditionally elitist connotations of tea in France, these salons are the opposite of noisy, working-class bistros, and they enable connoisseurs to savor fine teas in peace and comfort—indeed, intimacy—in surroundings unmarked by the march of time. Unlike cafés (those perfect symbols of French conviviality, the preferred meeting place of artists and intellectuals), tea rooms were long thought to be "tepid, draft-proof homes for old people," in Roland Jaccard's words. And it is true that their often old-fashioned charm is more

353. PARIS — Bois de Boulogne
Le Restaurant de la Cascade C. M.

"Odette poured Swann 'his' tea and asked, 'Milk or lemon?' And since he answered, 'Milk,' she laughingly said, 'A drop!' and then, since he found it good, 'So you see that I know what you like.' That tea, in fact, seemed like a precious thing to Swann, and . . . during the entire trip back in his coupé . . . he repeated to himself, 'It would be jolly pleasant to have a little lady at whose place one could find that ever so rare thing, good tea.'" Marcel Proust, *Un amour de Swann. Above:* Tea time at the Restaurant de la Cascade in the Bois de Boulogne, circa 1900. *Opposite:* A 1908 painting by G. Croegaert titled *In Private.*

conducive to melancholy and reverie than to social mingling and debate.

Yet this image is swiftly changing today, for France is one of the few countries in which the consumption of tea continues to grow—in fact it has doubled in the past thirty years. Every neighborhood in Paris, as well as the downtown area of every provincial city, boasts new and inviting tea rooms that are less strait-laced than their predecessors, thereby attracting an increasingly younger clientele. The French have always been interested in exploring exotic flavors, and by tradition they expect authentic, high-quality gastronomy. The better tea rooms thus enable them to discover an infinite variety of teas. And French retailers now offer these new gourmets what is perhaps the widest range of refined blends

"The day I noted down a conversation with Vincent that I had so enjoyed, we had gone for tea near Saint-Séverin, to the English pub that has such good lemon pies. It wasn't to reward him, for he in no way deserved it. It was because we wanted quite simply to talk. Vincent was eleven years old." In this excerpt from *La Maison de papier*, F. Mallet-Joris is referring to the Tea Caddy, the most British of Paris tea rooms. *Above:* Other Parisian tea salons include Le Loir dans la Théière and Les Contes de Thés. *Opposite:* The interior decor at Angelina has been officially listed as being of historic interest.

and scented teas in the world. Customers today flock to certain Parisian tea shops to buy a few of the three hundred teas listed in the catalogue, all sold in bulk so that they can be sniffed prior to purchase (unless, of course, the customer prefers cotton muslin teabags in which even excellent teas can steep in dignity). In such shops, all blends are composed of the finest harvests, and only natural essences are used to scent flavored teas.

French savoir-faire in tea has thus become synonymous with strict standards and quality, and is now being exported along with champagne and haute couture. Strange signs of the times include seeing a member of the British royal family in the London branch of a French tea merchant, and witnessing customers in Tokyo department stores flock to buy "French tea."

Today, tea is under pressure from the massive invasion of soft drinks. Industrial manufacturers of tea, responding to the new soft-drink habits, have stressed over the past twenty years the sale of teabags and, to a lesser extent, powdered instant and ready-made teas. This concession to modern life-style has spurred several countries such as Indonesia to sacrifice its fine harvest in favor of a poorer quality of mass-produced tea. On the other hand, choosing not to fight on the Coca-Cola front, many tea merchants, particularly those in France, have decided to help a growing number of consumers discover and appreciate all the subtlety of the precious nectar. The success of this approach means that demand for quality teas now outstrips supply, once again encouraging tea-growing countries to carefully cultivate their gardens. Thus, even if the continued rise in the consumption of tea is due to mass-produced goods, it is thanks to the revival of an art that a growing number of connoisseurs are acquiring the true savoir-faire associated with tea time.

French enthusiasm for tea goes beyond fine tea shops and salons. Silver-smiths and leather craftsmen also contribute to the French concept of tea as an *art de vivre*. Elegant wicker baskets complete with thermos and full tea service brought picnic teas back into fashion. *Above:* The Vuitton firm designed this travel case for taking tea in style anywhere. In the 1880s, the Christofle company offered an exclusive blend of smoky China tea to buyers of a new line of silver teaware inlaid with ebony. *Opposite:* Jean-Louis Dumas-Hermès, a paragon of Parisian elegance, sips his favorite tea from a Limoges china cup.

THE TASTE

·OF TEA·

Catherine Donzel

"English tea or China tea?" This is the question Asian waiters invariably ask of European tourists sitting, say, in the early-morning shade of a large green and white awning on the terrace of the Raffles Hotel in Singapore, or beneath the gilded stucco decorating the lobby of the Peninsula Hotel in Hong Kong. If travelers opt for the first choice, breakfast will be served with rather strong black tea, probably from Ceylon, in a teabag. Since it will have steeped too long in the teapot, milk will have to be added to mask the bitterness. Yet if guests choose "China tea" out of curiosity, they may well note a bemused glint in the waiter's eye. The hotel employee knows full well that Western tourists will probably be surprised by the tea they have just ordered. For instance, it might turn out to be a semifermented whole-leaf tea known as Oolong, a pale brew with a refreshing and flowery flavor. Some disconcerted Westerners may then attempt, unsuccessfully, to evoke a more familiar flavor by adding milk and sugar. This is heresy in the eyes of the Chinese waiter, who will nevertheless refrain from voicing his disapproval of the all-too-common faux pas. Yet such ignorance is comparable to that of rich Asians who spoil fine cognac by adding fizzy water.

For decades, Western tea drinkers have marched to a British tune. Previously, of course, people knew that numerous varieties of tea existed, and that each had its own special taste. In the late seventeenth century, Europe drank green tea, the first kind to be imported. One hundred years later, all of Europe from Saint Petersburg to Paris delighted in the sweet and aromatic flavor of black China teas, avidly consuming "flowery teas" and "scented teas."

Elsewhere, subsequently famous teas such as the "caravan tea" carried across the Gobi desert from China into Russia initially seduced generations of connoisseurs thanks to its marked flavor of adventure. Starting in 1850, however, Western tastes in tea became progressively standardized, and only a few refined and curious palates managed to hold out against uniformity. England began growing tea in its colonies and eventually established a monopoly over the tea trade, ultimately managing to impose its own criteria on the rest of the Western world—the only tea worthy of the name was henceforth the strong, robust, deep amber variety from Ceylon or Assam. Major British firms marketed this perfectly uniform product on

"Nowhere is the English genius of domesticity more notably evidenced than in the festival of afternoon tea," declared George Gissing (1857-1903) in *The Private Papers of Henry Ryecroft.* "One of the shining moments of my day is that when, having returned a little weary from an afternoon walk, I exchange boots for slippers, out-of-doors coat for easy, familiar, shabby jacket, and, in my deep, soft-elbowed chair, await the tea-tray. . . ." *Above:* Late nineteenth-century French metal tea container with raised painted design. *Opposite:* Early morning tea served at an inn in the Cotswolds, England. *Page 196:* Preparing cups of tea for a professional tasting session at the London Centre of the Tea Trade.

an international scale. They did this so thoroughly that many Westerners considered these strong blends of India teas to be the only valid point of reference. This opinion is still held by many people today, even though it completely disregards the rich universe of tea. When one realizes that there are more kinds of tea in China than there are wines in France, that each local plot of land produces a tea unlike any other, that the flavor of Darjeeling changes as the seasons change, and that the bud and open leaf on any given tea branch have differing properties, one begins to realize why it is such a shame to cling to a narrow view of tea.

Openly exploring the wide range of flavors produced by teas from India, Japan, China and Africa, however, requires a great deal of care and discrimination. There is not only a tea for every taste, but also for every moment of the day. Some outstanding teas can be compared to great vintage wines, whereas other perfectly worthy yet more conventional teas are to be drunk daily like decent table wines. This is why white tea, one of the most exclusive varieties in the world, should really be tasted only if one is already a connoisseur. To a less experienced palate, the crystal-clear liquid made from these pretty, velvety buds will simply appear bland—an expensive mistake to make, given the price of white tea!

Similarly, people accustomed to strong, full-bodied teas have to adapt gradually to green or semifermented teas with delicate, subtle flavors. At first, for instance, a spoonful or two of such teas can be added to a normal blend, or they can be sampled with food chosen to enhance their character. It would seem, moreover, that consumers follow this

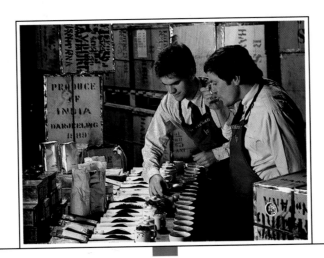

Until the Second World War, most of the European tea trade passed not only through London but also Amsterdam, which boasted a major auction center. Currently, continental Europe buys much of its international supply of tea in Hamburg. During the auctions that still govern 75 percent of the tea trade, buy orders depend entirely on tea tasters. They must work swiftly as well as accurately, since the quality of the shipments is judged by samples tasted just prior to auction. *Above:* A professional tasting session in Hamburg. *Opposite:* A tea merchant in Kurseong, Bengal.

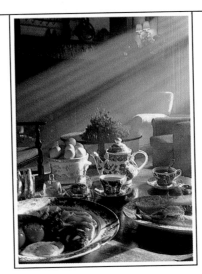

progressive initiation almost naturally. In France, for example, the scented teas that were in vogue in the 1970s produced a new generation of connoisseurs. Scented teas are in fact an ideal starting point because they familiarize tea drinkers with both standard and exotic flavors, and then lead bit by bit to an interest in more refined aromas. Tea drinkers evolve almost unconsciously from a taste for flowers and fruit to a taste for tea.

The tea leaf itself bears the traits of the soil in which it was grown. Each harvest has its own special quality, whether cultivated on the plains, in the mountains, on Himalayan slopes in springtime or in Ceylon during a hot summer. Each cup of tea represents an imaginary voyage. The names of the various regions alone conjure up distant lands, and the names of gardens are even more evocative. It is probable that many customers occasionally purchase one tea rather than another simply because of the exotic, enchanting appeal of the name on one of those large, painted tins lining the retailer's shelves. Good tea merchants are obviously aware of this effect, for they shrewdly invent attractive names for house blends and newly imported varieties.

In China, the practice of numbering the main types of tea is used for foreigners only, since merchants employ an anthology of poetic and picturesque names to entice local consumers. China tea is rarely labeled only by province or place of origin. The countless varieties of China tea are named after flowers, rivers, mythological heroes and celestial divinities, not to mention the all-powerful Black Dragon clan so popular in "the land of ten thousand teas."

Magical-sounding names constitute one of the charms of drinking tea. But they can also be a source of error and confusion for less experienced aficionados. Before wandering into the maze of gardens and pluckings (a field that requires solid bearings), it is better to decide exactly what pleasure or stimulation is being sought from a cup of tea. Breakfast normally calls for a strong, full-bodied tea, whereas a light, digestive variety is a better way to round off lunch. A refreshing, vitamin-rich drink may serve as a thirst-quencher throughout the day, while a mild, scented, low-theine tea is ideal in the evening. Indeed, there are teas for all seasons. One need merely become familiar with the major categories defined by European tasters to

Above: Yorkshire is the English county perhaps most attached to British tea-drinking traditions. "High tea" there might include smoked fish and soft-boiled eggs. *Left:* High-handled Chinese teapots. Similarly shaped vessels were also used in China to pour wine. *Opposite:* The "Tee Import" shop in Basel, Switzerland, and its current owner. The establishment was founded in the eighteenth century by an importer of china porcelain, becoming Switzerland's first tea shop.

identify the various characteristics of black, green and semifermented teas.

Well before Westerners decided to bring a little order to the cluttered world of tea, the Chinese had already established the broad outlines of their own classification system. The Chinese system is based essentially on the color of the liquor—red, green, white or yellow. It requires such

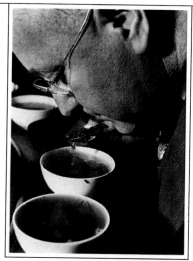

sophisticated knowledge of tea that it was never adopted by Europeans. In the West, teas were classified solely by country of origin (India, China, Ceylon, et cetera) until roughly 1945. Indicating the place of origin, however, is not sufficient to describe the flavor of a tea. Many tea rooms in France, for instance, list "China tea" on the menu. This is meaningless in itself, and simply indicates that the term "China" now refers only to smoky teas from the Fujian region, thereby obscuring the fact that China also produces unsmoked black teas, semifermented teas, and a wide range of green teas. "Ceylon" and "Assam" are also the object of rather hasty generalizations. These strong and stimulating morning teas can sometimes be quite delicate and thus appropriate for a soothing cup of afternoon tea. The difference is found in the leaf—that is to say, whether the leaves are whole or broken.

That is why Western experts have employed a new classification system for the past fifty years, a system that takes the degree of fermentation into account, along with manufacturing processes and the "grade" of the tea as determined by the size and form of the leaves. Taken together, these criteria constitute a rich palette of specific flavors, enabling tea drinkers to choose their variety according to taste or mood.

In describing the characteristics of tea, professional tasters employ a vocabulary as picturesque as that used by wine-tasters. Thus a tea leaf with fine appearance is "well-twisted"; if too large for the grade to which it is assigned, it is described as "bold." An immature tea tastes "green," whereas a fully "mature" tea is neither bitter nor flat. *Top:* A member of the U.S. Board of Tea Experts in a tasting session in New York, 1940. *Above:* A china cup, an English teapot, and a Chinese tea container. *Opposite:* Teas lining the shelves of the Mariage Frères boutique in Paris.

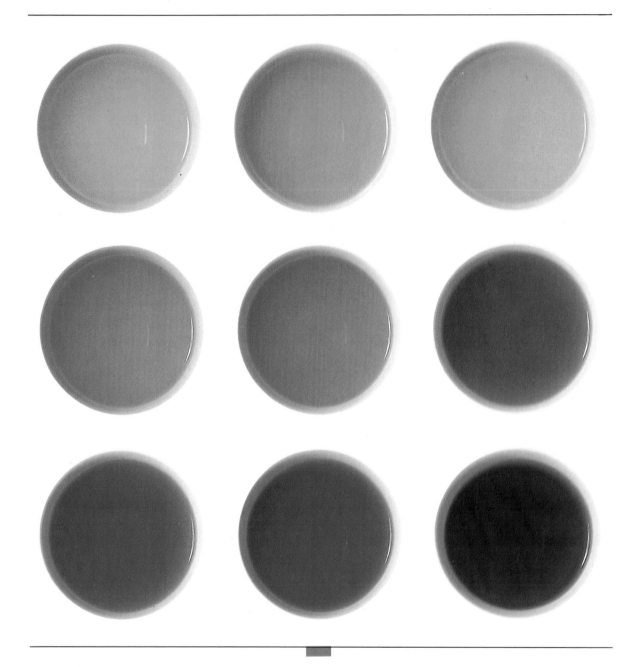

"Relatives were invited to sample the teas. . . . They began with the most delicate teas, the China teas that retain a subtle scent of lacquer, the almost colorless teas from Formosa with their flowery taste, the somewhat orangey Orange Pekoes, and the subtle Russian teas. . . ." Jacques Chardonne, *Les Destinées sentimentales. Above, left to right, top to bottom:* The color of tea—Yin Zhen (white China tea), Lung Ching (green China tea), Sencha Honyama (green Japan tea), Ti Kuan Yin (semifermented Formosa tea), T.G.F.O.P. "first flush" Darjeeling, Ceylon Orange Pekoe, Darjeeling Broken Pekoe Souchong, Uva Highlands B.O.P. (Ceylon), B.O.P. Fannings (Cameroon).

COLOR AND FLAVOR

According to legend, black tea was produced by chance, in the hold of an East India Company ship transporting green China tea that accidently fermented during the crossing. Whereupon Europeans, immediately attracted to the aroma of the fortuitous product, convinced the Chinese to manufacture this new type of tea. The anecdote obviously has no basis in fact, but it accurately conveys the truth that black tea is a typically Western taste that appeals less to an Oriental palate, which is traditionally more sensitive to the subtle aromas of green and semifermented teas. For that matter, black tea is mass produced only in those countries where Westerners themselves planted the crop—India, Ceylon, and Africa. Japan produces no fermented tea, and China exports almost all of its black tea.

Europeans acquired a taste for black tea along with the taste for sweets. The full, round aroma of **black tea** married very well, in fact, with sweet flavors; moreover, it was the only tea that could tolerate—on occasion—a drop of milk. As to the golden brown color of black tea, it naturally appealed to people accustomed to admiring the red, maroon and ochre hues of wine and beer. These colors were more familiar to Europeans than the pale pink or jade green of Oriental brews.

Once beyond such generalizations, however, it quickly becomes clear that not all black teas are alike. The secret of their diversity is encoded in several obscure initials usually written just after the country of origin. Thus B.O.P., G.F.O.P. or even F.T.G.F.O.P. seen in a catalogue or on a container simply indicates the degree of maturity and the form of the tea leaf.

Among whole-leaf black teas, the most subtle quality is called Flowery Orange Pekoe (F.O.P.). It refers to teas harvested early and carefully, composed only of unopened buds and the first two leaves beneath the bud. The word Pekoe comes from the Chinese *Pak-ho*, which alludes to the fine hair of a newborn infant and, by association, was applied to young tea buds still covered with a light down. "Orange," contrary to popular belief, has nothing to do with color or flavor, but refers to the princes of Orange descended from the house of Nassau—it thus conveys the idea of noble quality and was probably first used by Dutch merchants. The leaves of a Flowery Orange Pekoe are easily identifiable and highly attractive. They are finely rolled lengthwise and interspersed with the golden tips of the buds. The more tips there are, the more expensive the tea. The grades of excellence move up through Golden Flowery Orange Pekoe (G.F.O.P.) to Finest Tippy Golden Flowery Orange Pekoe (F.T.G.F.O.P), yielding light, clear teas

"Tea is drunk to forget the din of the world," wrote Chinese sage T'ien Yiheng. *Following double page:* Tea utensils in modern-day China. (1) Lined basket for keeping the teapot warm. (2) Tea service dating from the beginning of this century. (3) Semifermented jasmine tea. (4) Pewter tea caddy. (5-6-8) Sundry packages of semifermented tea, including (7) a metal tin. (9-11) Round cakes of compressed tea. (10) A caddy from the Fook Ming Tong shop in Hong Kong.

composed almost entirely of tips. This type of leaf, wherever it comes from, will never produce a very strong brew; to the contrary, it makes an extremely fine and aromatic drink. Depending on the time of harvest—notably in Darjeeling—it may display a subtlety comparable to the great semifermented teas. Flowery Orange Pekoe is an ideal afternoon tea, as is Orange Pekoe (O.P.), which is the product of an equally careful but somewhat later harvest. At this stage of growth, the tea no longer has light tips and the leaves are longer and more elegant.

There are other sorts of whole-leaf black teas issued from less fine plucking methods, but they are not usually sold as such. Thus Pekoe, which is the product of the third leaf on the branch, is generally used in blends. Souchong, with dark leaves that are large and thick, is used in smoky teas such as Lapsang Souchong and Tarry Souchong.

For the strength and tannic acid taste usually sought in an early-morning cup of tea, a brew made from broken leaves is more appropriate. Contrary to common belief, broken-leaf teas are not necessarily inferior to whole-leaf teas. They have simply undergone a transformation process designed to make the tea stronger.

The finest broken-leaf teas, Broken Orange Pekoe, are made from high-quality harvests and may contain golden tips when made from Flowery Orange Pekoe. Such teas can be quite expensive, for they may require fairly sophisticated manufacturing processes.

Teas labeled "Dust" or "Fannings" are made of crushed leaves, and produce an even stronger beverage with greater body. These teas are usually sold in teabags, for they consist of tiny pieces of leaf.

Broken-leaf, dust and fannings can withstand a drop of milk and a little sugar—should the tea-drinker insist on them.

Green tea is worlds away from black tea. Dark liquors and the taste of tannic acid give way to pale hues and refreshing aromas as the scene shifts from European dining tables to Buddhist temples. Sugary tea parties and robust breakfasts have been left far behind. The classification system so well adapted to Western tastes is of no use in the East. In the land of green tea, the concepts of body and strength are not relevant, and the various "grades" of leaf (which, in the case of black tea, indicate relative strength) have little meaning. For that matter, with the exception of a powdered green tea produced in Japan ("Matcha"), unfermented teas are always whole-leaf teas. Those sold in the West are usually the product of the finest harvests. Local techniques of cultivation and manufacture, on the other hand, yield a wide variety of aromas. Thus green teas from China and Formosa are strikingly different from the teas produced according to Japanese methods.

"Even as the difference in favorite vintages marks the separate idiosyncracies of different periods and nationalities of Europe, so the Tea-ideals characterize their various moods of Oriental culture." Kakuzo Okakura, *The Book of Tea. Opposite:* Japanese tea merchants choosing teas offered by an American firm doing business in Japan. This selection probably involves black tea, since Japan, which exports only a little green tea, imports a sizable amount of fermented tea.

Better-quality China teas are generally sold as flat leaves of a fine verdigris color, or silvery in the case of superior teas such as Dong Yang Dong Bai, composed exclusively of downy buds and very young leaves. The color of the liquid itself is crystalline, varying from orange-green to pale pink. The taste is mild and subtle. The leaves of other qualities of tea, less prized by the Chinese, are carefully rolled into a ball. Hyson, for example, a green tea drunk widely during the nineteenth century, is rolled into fine pearls; gunpowder, on the other hand, is rolled into larger, regular balls (this is the variety that is mixed with fresh mint to make the mint tea drunk in Muslim countries).

Japan produces only green tea, of which there are numerous varieties. Only a few kinds are exported, however, the rest being consumed locally. These unusually refreshing teas superbly recreate the organic harmony of the gardens in which they were grown. Japanese tea leaves are greener and more vivid in color than China tea, and the liquor is stronger in hue, going from jade green to light yellow. The taste evokes the aromatic strength of freshly cut herbs. Westerners are generally surprised by Japanese tea. It requires an educated palate to savor the rare delights of Gyokuro ("Precious Dew"), whose buds, three weeks prior to plucking, are shielded by a large black canvas, an operation designed to increase their chlorophyll content and intensify their dark green hue. Similarly, experience is required to truly appreciate a grand Matcha Uji, which comes in the form of a jade-green powder that is whipped in a little pure water and yields a magnificent, concentrated, nourishing beverage. It is more sensible to begin by sampling Sencha teas, which are excellent yet less sophisticated than the previous two. Bancha teas are also a good place to start, since they are produced for everyday use in Japan, not unlike European table wines.

A green tea is judged on its aroma, which must be highly developed, and on the length of its taste in the mouth. Great Japanese teas are recognizable from the way they fill the palate with an enduring, fragrant, slightly sweet flavor. Green tea sometimes tends to be bitter. This may be considered a drawback by some, even though the bitter taste—which is one of the features of tea in general—is often highly appreciated. Whatever the case, the bitterness can be eliminated by rinsing green tea in water prior to steeping. Unfermented teas must be drunk straight, without milk or sugar. They make a pleasant accompaniment to a meal, thanks to their digestive properties. They are gentle teas that can be drunk throughout the day; given their high vitamin C content, however, they are not recommended in the evening. Although not an excitant, green teas have a revitalizing effect and are

"When all is complete deep in the teapot, when tea, mint, and sugar have completely diffused throughout the water, coloring and saturating it . . . then a glass will be filled and poured back into the mixture, blending it further. Then comes waiting. Motionless waiting. Finally, from high up, like some green cataract whose sight and sound mesmerize, the tea will once again cascade into a glass. Now it can be drunk, dreamily, forehead bowed, fingers held wide away from the scalding glass." Simone Jacquemard, *Le mariage berbère*. *Opposite:* Mint tea and oriental pastries.

also reputed to be an intellectual stimulant.

A tea leaf should "have creases like leathern boot of Tatar horsemen, curl like the dewlap of a mighty bullock, unfold like a mist rising out of a ravine." This image of the ideal leaf is taken from Kakuzo Okakura's translation of Lu Yu's seventh-century *Chaking*, the bible of tea. It is a good description of **semifermented teas**. Bulky, always whole and never rolled, such tea comes in a vast range of extravagant forms—the wiry coil of the legendary dragon, the quick-frozen flight of an insect, the angry arch of the eyebrow of a Chinese actor (one semifermented tea even draws its name from this visual analogy). Semifermented tea undergoes only an initial fermentation process and therefore combines the aromas of black and green teas. Smoother than black tea, less fresh and grassy than green tea, semifermented tea displays a certain balance and harmony.

Known by the generic name of Oolong, the various types of semifermented tea can be divided into two main groups. One includes the so-called China Oolong teas, rarely exported, that have undergone 12 to 20 percent of the fermentation process. These teas are common in China and have a very "Oriental" taste reminiscent of spring vegetation. They produce a pale yellow liquor. The second major group—Formosa Oolong teas—undergoes longer fermentation (approximately 60 percent) and produces a golden brew with a more "Occidental" flavor. Among the teas of this latter type normally consumed in Europe is one called Oriental Beauty, also known in France as Black Dragon (the literal translation of *Oolong*). This is the most highly prized semifermented tea, as reflected in its price. It is generally described as having a taste of orchids, and is much appreciated by those who prefer Darjeeling and other light, aromatic teas.

Semifermented tea can be drunk throughout the day, and goes well with meals (apart from breakfast, which may require a stronger tea). It is low in theine, and is therefore perfect before bedtime, especially when steeped with jasmine, orange flowers, rose petals or other flowers known to have a calming effect.

Opposite: Afternoon in an indoor garden. The tea is served in Wedgwood china, whose characteristic two-color Greek pattern was designed in the 1830s. *Preceding double page:* (1) Cast-iron Japanese brazier used in the tea ceremony. (2) Ancient Japanese cast-iron kettle. (3) Chinese tea service including a cup with cover (*chung*) used to brew a single cup of tea. (4) Metal tea caddy, 1900. (5) Nineteenth-century tea caddy in brass. (6) Nineteenth-century brass samovar from Russia. (7-8) Packages of China tea. (9) An eighteenth-century merchant's tea container. (10) Tea caddy, early twentieth century. (11) Porcelain tea service from Japan, circa 1900.

HOW TO PREPARE TEA

Knowing how to choose the right tea is not enough. Tea from a great garden, composed of elegant-looking leaves that give off a wonderful aroma, may nevertheless prove to be disappointingly dull in the cup. In fact, it often happens that customers of exclusive tea shops will angrily return to the counter after having bought a superb tea, complaining that the brew did not live up to its promise and that the highly vaunted tea was not good. In most cases, however, it would be truer to say that it was the water or the teapot that was not good, or that the steeping time was wrong. For fully half of the success of tea depends on the care with which it is prepared.

First of all, the teapot—which is the tea-drinker's most precious "tool"—must be appropriate to the task, and be treated with respect. It should never be washed or scrubbed, but simply rinsed with running water and left to dry, uncovered, in the open air. This is designed to retain the deposit of tannin that coats the sides of the teapot little by little, for a natural lining enhances the flavor of tea

brewed in the pot. A highly "seasoned" teapot used for very strong or smoky teas, however, will retain their odor and should therefore not be used for mild, subtle teas. This is why, ideally, a serious tea-drinker should have a different teapot for each type of tea. Short of beginning an extensive teapot collection, however, three will suffice—one for strong tea, one for mild tea, and a third for scented teas. A terracotta or silver-plated teapot is well-suited to strong teas rich in tannin, such as Ceylon and Assam teas. Apparently pewter also gives excellent results for such teas, as does cast iron. Plain cast iron is appreciated by the Japanese because it releases extremely beneficial mineral salts, but it requires special care. Enameled cast iron, on the other hand, like porcelain and fine china, makes an ideal teapot for green and semifermented teas, as well as for light black teas such as Darjeeling. The shape of the teapot is not important, provided that it is functional—the rest is simply a question of personal taste. Perhaps the most practical model is a porcelain teapot with a felt-lined metallic cover; made in England and Germany, it is usually very

"When there weren't many visitors on a Tuesday, tea was served in the sitting room itself. [Countess Sabine] called Vandeuvres over, and questioned him on the way the English made tea. He often went to England, where his horses raced. According to Vandeuvres, only the Russians knew how to make tea, and he gave her the recipe." Emile Zola, *Nana. Above:* A photograph by M. Jeziorowska, *Rebeka. Opposite:* A collection of teapots and cups in a Moscow apartment. Most of these are Russian, and date from the early nineteenth century.

attractive and offers the advantage of keeping tea at the right temperature for a long time.

It is too often overlooked that, in the final analysis, tea is merely flavored water, and that therefore the quality of the water must be taken into account. It is said that Chinese tea masters were able to recognize the specific water used to brew tea, whether it came from the edge of a river, from the middle of a running torrent, or from a deep well. Some extremely refined connoisseurs have highly reputed water shipped to them, and it is said that the queen of England never travels without a supply of spring water used to prepare her tea. On a more simple level, it is important to be sure that the water is pure, fresh, odorless and free of calcium. In some areas, urban tap water is naturally soft and perfectly appropriate. To check, boil a little water beforehand, then smell the steam to detect any potentially undesirable odors. Or simply use the water filters sold in many stores. A neutral mineral water, for instance one recommended for infants, is another good source.

After having selected teapot and water, it is at last time to brew the tea. First of all, heat water in a kettle preferably used only for preparing tea. The teapot should be thoroughly warmed before the tea leaves are placed in it, being careful to use the right amount. One can generally figure 2.5 grams of tea per cup, which is approximately one rounded teaspoon. This measure applies most accurately to whole, black tea leaves; for broken leaves, a level teaspoon is enough, and for fannings, two-thirds of a teaspoon will suffice. A good cup of Oolong, on the other hand, requires two good spoonfuls of tea leaves. The proper dose for green tea varies according to the type in question; in general, one can reckon on three grams per cup, but the tea merchant's advice is important here.

Once placed in the bottom of the thoroughly heated teapot, the leaves should be left there for a minute or two, wrapped in the ambient steam, for only then will the full aroma be released.

"Dear, do you think the water has boiled enough to be poured over the tea?"

"I think, dearest, that it is still too soon."

Too late is more like it. When Madame de Staël penned this dialogue in *Corinne*, she was apparently unaware that water for tea should never be allowed to boil, for this will make it flat and lifeless. Furthermore, if too hot, it will harm the tea leaves and alter their flavor. The water should be poured on the leaves when it is barely simmering. Everything then becomes a question of time. Black tea should be steeped from three minutes (broken leaves) to five minutes (whole leaves). Semifermented teas require seven minutes to bring out their best flavor. Green tea from Japan is brewed for one or two minutes, whereas China tea requires

"The room was well furnished and scrupulously clean, and there was a wood fire in the grate. Given a chair at a gate-legged table on which the miller's wife spread a spotless, beautifully laundered cloth, Mrs. Bradley gazed out of the window at the denuded trees and the grey autumn sky. Her hostess returned with tea, scones, butter and jam and informed her that 'the girl' was attending to 'the gentleman' in the car." Gladys Mitchell, *The Greenstone Griffins*, 1983. *Opposite, top:* Afternoon tea. *Opposite, bottom:* A commemorative teapot portraying Queen Victoria and Prince Albert. *Following double page:* (1) Solid silver eighteenth-century tea caddy. (2, 4) Tea chests of fine inlaid wood. (5) Traditional British teapot. (6) Chinese bamboo strainer. (3,7) Nineteenth-century household tea caddies made of tin. (8) Early nineteenth-century engraved pewter tea caddy.

three to five minutes, but once again variations exist and the advice of a competent salesperson is useful.

Stir well prior to serving and, above all, remove the leaves once the tea has steeped. Nothing is gained, except added bitterness, from letting the tea brew longer, despite a rather widely held belief that the longer a tea is steeped the more stimulating and rich in theine it will be. This is untrue, for theine is released in the first minute of brewing, after which the increased presence of tannins will tend to counter its effect.

If the teapot has a built-in strainer, simply lift it out to remove the leaves. If not, a strainer made of cotton (the most appropriate material) may be used, to be removed when the tea is ready to serve. Tea balls are also convenient, but must be rather large in order to provide enough space for the tea to swell, since leaves double in volume once plunged into water.

Obviously, it is not always possible to follow every rule to the letter when making a cup of tea. That is no reason, however, to deprive oneself of a good cup of tea at the office, for example. This is where teabags of muslin (not paper!) come in handy. Good tea merchants sell teabags of a quality comparable to loose tea. Unfortunately, it is very difficult to find green and semifermented teas packaged this way.

There is no point in trying to save time by buying a large quantity of tea in advance. It is a fragile and precious commodity, and must be stored in an airtight box or jar, away from dampness and light, for a limited period only—twelve months for black teas, six to

The earliest tea caddies were imported from China and Japan, and were originally simple terracotta jars with a cover used to measure out the tea. Since tea was a costly item in Europe, caddies soon became small chests complete with lock, to which only the mistress of the house held the key. Such caddies normally had two compartments (for green and black tea) plus a dish in which teas could be blended or sugar stored (sugar being another expensive commodity). *Above:* Tea caddies. *Opposite:* English teapots of glazed clay with pewter tops.

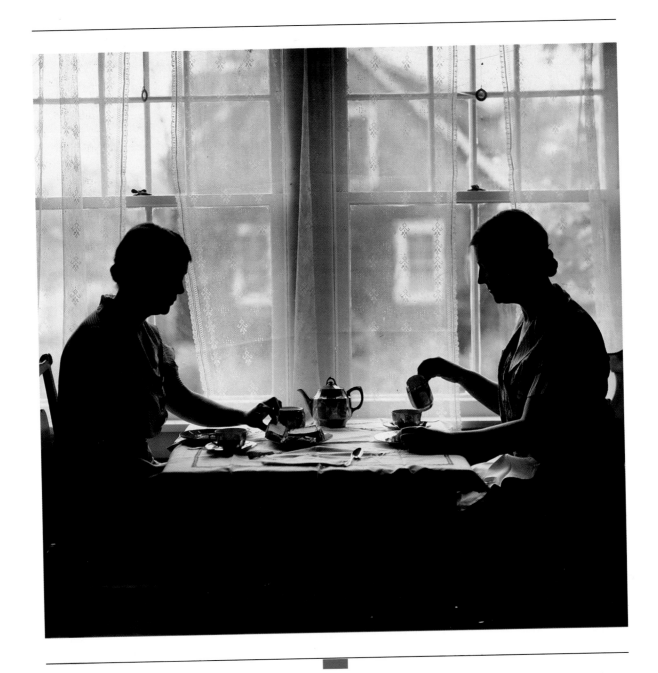

"She was a fine woman, a perfect gentlewoman. She had taken life, as she liked a cup of tea—weak, with an exquisite aroma and plenty of cream and sugar." Henry James, "De Grey: A Romance," 1868. *Above:* Two Americans enjoying five o'clock tea in 1930. *Preceding double page:* (1) A 1925 teapot. (2) An infuser. (3) Teaspoons. (4) Tea-flavored jelly. (5) Porcelain infuser for a single cup of tea. (6,7) 1930s-style tea service. (8) Rock sugar. (9) Muslin teabags.

eight months for semifermented and green teas (which the Japanese store in the refrigerator). If tea is purchased in a supermarket, the final sale date should be checked.

There remains the thorny question of milk, sugar and lemon. For "true" connoisseurs, it is a sacrilege to employ such additives. This hard line may be softened, however, to satisfy all tastes.

Thus, as mentioned above, certain teas "tolerate" a drop of cold milk. In general, this applies to the strong, full-bodied black teas in broken-leaf form, such as those from Assam, Ceylon, and Indonesia. In short, it might be said that milk is suitable—perhaps—for morning teas. But for lighter teas of the Darjeeling type, as well as for smoky, green and semifermented teas, milk is absolutely unacceptable. Lemon, which changes both the taste and color of tea, is to be banned in all cases. A thin slice of orange, on the other hand, can sometimes enhance the aroma of an Assam or Ceylon tea.

Sugar, if one insists on adding it, should be neutral white rock sugar (in Britain, "candy" sugar), preferably to be used only in average-quality black tea. It might be pointed out that the flavor of sugar does marry well with scented teas, as they are already a kind of dessert.

Nevertheless, sugar and milk will always encounter staunch opponents, as reflected in a passage from an article by George Orwell in which he claimed that adding sugar to tea was like adding salt or pepper. He compared the natural astringency of tea to the pleasant bitterness of English beer, and pointed out that if one really wanted a sweet drink, the most sensible thing to do would be to melt sugar in hot water. Not everyone's cup of tea!

Steeping tea in an elegant teapot and sipping it from a charming cup was long a luxury reserved for the privileged classes. But by the 1850s, the invention of electroplating techniques (which allowed for the infinite reproduction of a metallic object) and the mass production of ceramics put a tea service within reach of most people. Furthermore, this alliance of art and industry has meant that fine tea accessories can be periodically re-manufactured. Thus perfect reproductions of tea services designed for use on glamorous ocean liners or in palaces are now for sale, enabling connoisseurs to add a drop of fantasy to their tea. *Above:* A photograph by Michel Dubois titled *Hollywood 1932*, included in a limited-edition book on tea published at the initiative of Damman Frères.

GREAT TEA REGIONS AND TRADITIONAL BLENDS

The processing, maturity and form of the leaf give tea its taste—the region in which it was grown gives it its character. Original features associated with each estate mean that all the major classes of tea can be endlessly subdivided and distinguished. Yet some districts produce teas that are inevitably prestigious, thanks to a combination of favorable climate and tried-and-tested cultivation techniques. The most famous of these exclusive teas come from just five countries—Ceylon (Sri Lanka), China, Formosa (Taiwan), India and Japan.

Kitti Cha Sangmanee, expert tea-taster, scours the globe for rare teas and creates exclusive blends for Mariage Frères in Paris.

C e y l o n

Ceylon, that "island of tea," basically produces black tea known for its aromatic amber liquor and its rich, full, astringent flavor. It goes very well with a little cold milk and harmoniously accompanies a sweet breakfast or afternoon pastry. Ceylonese estates all produce a tea of particular flavor but they are too numerous to be listed. It is more useful here to classify the island's tea according to the grades of leaf, progressing from

1 - CEYLON F.O.P.

2 - CEYLON O.P.

3 - CEYLON B.O.P.

4 - KEEMUN F.O.P.

5 - LAPSANG SOUCHONG

the mildest to the strongest. A famous estate or two is listed under each grade.

Flowery Orange Pekoe. Very attractive leaves with golden tips that give a flavorful, mellow brew of great distinction. Estates that produce fine F.O.P.s include Berubeula and Allen Valley. An afternoon tea.

Orange Pekoe. Tea with long, thin leaves, fruitier than F.O.P. The Pettiagalla and Kenilworth estates produce remarkable O.P. tea. An afternoon tea.

Flowery Pekoe. The liquor is both full and aromatic. A well-balanced tea, with fine estates in Dyraaba and Uva Highlands. A morning and afternoon tea.

Broken Orange Pekoe. In this category, teas from Saint James, Dimbula and Uva Highlands are noted for being flavory and full, with great character. A morning tea.

Broken Orange Pekoe Fannings. These teas are so full-bodied that they are a good substitute for coffee. A drop of cold milk, merely tolerated in the above grades, is strongly recommended here, for milk marries marvelously well with fannings. The Uva Highlands and Dyraaba estates produce fine fannings. A morning and after-meal tea.

A young tea picker in Ceylon (Sri Lanka). In her right hand she holds the delicate terminal stem gathered during a "fine plucking"—just two top leaves and the leaf-bud, or "tip."

C h i n a

BLACK TEAS FROM CHINA are mild and low in theine, and therefore considered perfect afternoon and evening teas. With the exception of Yunnan, they are never taken with milk or sugar.

Keemun. This type of tea is not smoky, and is known for its orchid aroma and brilliant red liquor. Its mild, sweet flavor makes it a perfect evening tea. It is also frequently used as the base for scented blends.

Lapsang Souchong. This moderately smoky tea is produced by withering the leaves over open fires of pine. It goes well with salty and spicy dishes, and with cheese.

Yunnan. This non-smoky tea comes in G.F.O.P. and T.G.F.O.P grades, and is one of China's "noble" varieties. It is one of the rare teas to combine aroma with strength, subtlety with rich taste. Full and round, it is nicknamed "the mocha of tea." With a fine golden liquor and a taste that remains long in the mouth, Yunnan will tolerate a drop of milk and is perfect for a continental breakfast.

Compressed bricks of tea are used as follows: for each cup, break off and pulverize two grams of tea, place the powder in simmering water, steep for five minutes, stir, and strain or filter.

GREEN CHINA TEA, like that from Japan, should never be drunk with milk or sugar.

Dong Yang Dong Bai. One of the finest green teas in the world, it is noted for its flowery bouquet, its smooth, long-lasting taste and its clear liquor.

6 - YUNNAN T. G. F. O. P.

7 - DONG YANG DONG BAI

8 - LUNG CHING

9 - PI LO CHUN

10 - SILVER DRAGON

Lung Ching ("Dragon Well"). This famous tea yields a superb jade-colored liquor. Its exquisite flavor and delicate aroma are perfect any time of the day, but Lung Ching is particularly appreciated by those who need to stay up late since it is stimulating and is reputed to help keep the mind clear.

Pi Lo Chun ("Spiral of Spring Jade"). A fairly rare tea sold only by the finest tea dealers. Round and mild, it should be saved for grand occasions.

Silver Dragon. This tea owes its name to the silver down covering its leaves, whose shape suggests the silhouette of a dragon. It produces a light, limpid liquor of intense aroma and sweet taste. A daytime tea.

WHITE TEA is different from black, green and semifermented teas. It is difficult to obtain, for production is limited. White tea undergoes almost no transformation—once harvested, it is merely withered and dried. Its name, a literal translation from the Chinese, probably comes from the very pale color of its liquor. Moreover, high-quality white teas come in the form of white buds whose texture is comparable to the petals of the edelweiss flower. The subtle taste of white tea requires an experienced palate already initiated into the "Oriental" flavors of green and semifermented teas.

Yin Zhen ("Silver Needles"). This white tea is produced by the "imperial" plucking method, performed at dawn on only two days of the year. The beauty of its fine, silvery buds, its delicate and refreshing taste make it one of the most glamorous—and expensive—teas in the world. To be sampled, preferably, in summer.

Pai Mu Tan. This has a somewhat more ordinary quality than Yin Zhen, but the leaf can still be appreciated in its natural state, for it remains just as it was when plucked from the bush. Smooth and flowery, this is an appropriate tea for evening.

F o r m o s a

Tarry Souchong. Produced according to traditional Chinese methods, this is the most heavily smoked black tea of all. Reserved for aficionados of its special smoky flavor, Tarry Souchong makes a good accompaniment to hearty breakfasts and brunches.

Gunpowder. This green tea is rolled into little balls that "explode" when placed in the teapot. It is widely used to prepare mint tea, but is also delicious on its own. The yellow-green liquor is highly refreshing. A relaxing, afternoon tea.

SEMIFERMENTED TEAS have become the great specialty of the island of Formosa, where the

11 - YIN ZHEN

finest of them are produced. Their taste is generally more subtle than that of semifermented teas made in China. They are to be drunk plain, without milk, during or after a meal, at any time of day. They are low in theine and therefore also appropriate as an evening beverage.

Imperial Oolong. This is the finest tea from the family of Oriental Beauty (or Black Dragon) teas. The liquor is somewhat amber-colored and hints of chestnut and honey flavors. Highly aromatic, it is a fine evening tea.

Grand Pouchong. This is one of the family of China Oolongs that has undergone only slight fermentation. The liquor has a fine golden color, the delicate aroma yields a subtle flavor. A daytime or evening tea.

Ti Kuan Yin ("Iron Goddess of Mercy"). This tea is known for its digestive properties. The liquor is amber-hued, and it has a mild taste yet fully developed aroma.

Tung Ting. Another member of the China Oolong family, Tung Ting is one of the most famous Formosa teas. The liquor is orange-red, the flavor very mild. A daytime and evening tea.

Semifermented China tea sold in the form of a round cake of compressed leaves is steeped in small Chinese teapots of red clay.

I n d i a

Teas from India, like those from Ceylon, are black teas designed to satisfy "Western" tastes, and are therefore characterized by their full-bodied flavor and rich, deeply colored liquor. But India also produces a wide variety of black teas that are more subtle, and can be as delicate as semifermented teas from China and Formosa. India teas therefore offer a fine initiation into the taste of tea in general.

Assam. These are morning teas par excellence, with a strong, malty taste and dark liquor. They go well with a drop of cold milk. Assam boasts a number of famous gardens, including Thowra, Numalighur and Napuk. Tea drinkers nevertheless have a hard time distinguishing one garden from another since the tea is so strong.

Darjeeling. These are the rarest and most prestigious of black teas. They are generally sold in the best grade of whole leaves—G.F.O.P., T.G.F.O.P., and F.T.G.F.O.P. Highly esteemed gardens include Castleton, Bloomfield, Margaret's Hope, Namring and Gielle. Although it is rather difficult to distinguish one garden from another, the special flavor of each harvest period can be identified, for the taste of Darjeeling teas varies with the seasons. In general, these are afternoon teas taken plain, without milk (except when they are occasionally sold in broken-leaf form).

An Indian tea merchant poses beside chests decorated with elegant calligraphy.

First Flush Darjeeling. These are springtime teas, harvested from late February to mid-April. The young leaves yield a light tea with a flavor of green muscat. Their arrival is impatiently awaited by connoisseurs (not unlike the arrival of new Beaujolais wine), and they are sometimes specially airfreighted. A gentle, afternoon tea.

Second Flush Darjeeling. Harvested in May and June, these teas are more fully constructed than first flush varieties. The liquor is bright, the taste full and round with a fruity note. An afternoon tea.

In-Between Darjeeling. These intermediate teas are harvested in April and May, and combine the greenness of first flush teas with the maturity of second flush varieties.

Autumnal Darjeeling. These autumn-harvested Darjeelings are characterized by large leaves that give a round taste and coppery liquor. They can be drunk in the morning with a bit of cold milk.

Dooar. These are low-grown teas, dark and full-bodied, yet less strong than Assam teas. A daytime tea that goes well with a drop of milk.

Terai. Teas grown on the plain to the south of Darjeeling. The brew is richly colored, the taste spicy and liqueur-like. These teas can be drunk throughout the day and are often used in blends. They tolerate a bit of cold milk.

Travancore. Grown on the largest plantation in southern India, these teas produce a coppery liquor of strong, full-bodied flavor. They are intermediate teas that evoke teas from northern India while resembling Ceylon teas. A morning tea that may be taken with milk.

J a p a n

Japan produces only green tea. Low in theine yet unusually rich in vitamin C, these bracing and digestive teas are suitable beverages during and after meals. Yet they are also appropriate for a relaxing break. To be savored as is, without milk or sugar.

Genmaicha ("Japanese Rice"). A typically Japanese specialty—this medium-quality green tea is mixed with toasted rice and popped corn. To be sampled, out of curiosity, in the afternoon.

Gyokuro ("Precious Dew"). The flat, very green leaves of this tea are sharply pointed like pine needles and easily recognizable. This is the most refined of Japan teas—its liquor is greenish and its smooth taste remains long in the mouth. Given its cost, it is a tea to be drunk on special occasions.

Hojicha. A green tea that is roasted, producing brownish

21 · DOOARS T. G. F. O. P.

22 · TERAI T. G. F. O. P.

23 · TRAVANCORE F. B. O. P.

24 · GENMAICHA

25 · GYOKURO

leaves and liquor. Very light and low in theine, it pleasantly accompanies a meal.

Matcha Uji ("Froth of Liquid Jade"). Powdered tea made from Gyokuro leaves (although other, more common Matchas are made from less renowned leaves). In this specific case, Matcha Uji yields a jade green beverage that is concentrated and nourishing. It is perfect for making iced tea, as well as for coloring and flavoring sauces and sherbets.

Sencha Honyama. Like Gyokuro, this is one of Japan's great teas. It should be noted, however, that many types of Sencha exist, though few of them as prestigious as this one, with its pale green liquor, its fresh and flowery taste. A relaxing, afternoon tea.

TEA THE WORLD OVER

Starting in the nineteenth century, tea plantations spread across Asia and beyond, and began to be cultivated in regions of Africa, South America, the former Soviet Union, and the Near East. Production methods in these areas merit improvement,

A branch from a tea bush in flower, described in 1735 by J. B. Du Halde: "The flower is white, and has the form of a five-petaled rose. When the flowering season has passed, the plant produces berries that resemble a fleshy nut."

The Kuzmichev company has recently begun reusing the fine labels that adorned its containers of tea in the early 1900s. Gold dust is no longer used to embellish the labels, however, as it was in the days when Kuzmichev was purveyor to the top echelons of Saint Petersburg society.

for quantity is often placed above quality, as demonstrated by the mechanical harvesting techniques employed in the republic of Georgia. It must nevertheless be recognized that some "new" planters are now able to produce tea that rivals the finest varieties from India and Ceylon. It would therefore be a shame to deny oneself the pleasure of discovering them. At the English court, moreover, it is said that Her Majesty has become a fan of Cameroon tea—and it would hardly be proper to be more chauvinistic than the queen.

It should be noted that all the teas listed below are black teas; the cultivation and production of delicate green and semifermented teas remain the prerogative of countries possessing traditional, well-tested techniques.

ARGENTINA. Of medium body, tasting slightly of the local soil, these teas produce a dark liquor. They make an excellent morning tea and can be taken with a little cold milk.

BANGLADESH. The liquor is dark, the taste aromatic and slightly spicy. These are daytime teas, drunk with or without milk.

CAMEROON. High-quality, high-grown teas yielding a richly colored brew with an aromatic, malted taste. They can take a drop of cold milk and the broken-leaf grades in particular are perfect for the morning.

C.I.S. Russian tea is often

26 - HOJICHA

27 - MATCHA UJI

28 - SENCHA HONYAMA

29 - BANGLADESH G.F.O.P.

30 - CAMEROON F.B.O.P.

confused with "Imperial Russian" flavor, the latter being a blend of India and China teas flavored with citrus scents. "Real" Russian teas are generally grown in Georgia and are noted for their dark liquor, fairly full body and flowery taste. The whole-leaf grades produce decent afternoon or evening teas; the broken-leaf varieties are more appropriate in the morning, and can take a drop of cold milk.

MAURITIUS. These teas are characterized by their vanilla aroma. They are quite strong, go well with a little milk, and make a fine early-morning cup of tea.

INDONESIA. These teas are similar to those produced in Ceylon, for they are flavorful, fairly full and of a fine amber color. Perfect for the morning, particularly the broken-leaf grades. A little cold milk may be added to them.

IRAN. This tea makes a red brew that has all the lightness and mellowness of China teas. These afternoon teas are to be drunk plain.

KENYA. High-quality, Assam-like teas. Their liquor is golden, their flavor full and fruity. Perfect for the morning, with a drop of cold milk.

MALAYSIA. These broken-leaf teas produce a strong and forthright beverage appropriate for the morning, and can be taken with milk if desired.

NEPAL. The bright liquor of these teas, plus their fine, subtle and slightly fruity flavor,

A dried bouquet of green tea leaves bound together can be steeped directly in the cup, reviving the aroma and appearance of the fresh bouquet.

recall Darjeeling teas. To be taken plain, in the afternoon.

SIKKIM. High-quality teas grown on the high plateau of the Himalayas. Comparable to Darjeeling (to which they are geographically close), Sikkim teas nevertheless have more body and a hint of ripe fruit. The Temi gardens produce excellent Sikkim tea. An afternoon tea, to be appreciated as is.

TURKEY. The very mild, slightly sugary flavor of these teas recalls those of China. They come in whole-leaf grades to be drunk plain, in the evening.

CLASSIC BLENDS

Just as every wine owes its originality to a cellar master able to perfectly combine the qualities of various types of wine, so a tea taster must possess great skill in the art of blending. Tea tasters in the employ of major international retailers combine teas of various qualities to obtain a standardized product of predictable taste at a fixed price. These constitute the more "common" blends. Sometimes tea tasters act just like the "noses" of sophisticated perfume firms, inventing new blends that produce new aromas and thoroughly original tastes. This is done, for instance, by blending several great gardens from the same region to obtain a perfect

Didier Jumeau-Lafond, one of France's most knowledgeable tea experts.

31 - INDONESIA T.G.F.O.P.

32 - KENYA G.F.O.P.

33 - NEPAL G.F.O.P.

34 - SIKKIM T.G.F.O.P.

35 - TURKEY B.O.P.

balance of taste and color. Better still, the finest firms, by combining different types of tea from India to China, mixing black tea with green and fusing full-bodied and mild flavors, manage to produce teas whose origin cannot be pinpointed. This subtle alchemy makes every cup a delightful surprise.

The so-called "classic" blends that skillfully marry the aromas of various teas are the most difficult to produce—they are more subtle than the scented blends that simply sprinkle natural essences of flowers, leaves or fruit over the tea. With a little experience, however, a connoisseur can attempt a classic blend. There is no real recipe—a good scale, a healthy dose of intuition, and a few basic guidelines are all that are required. First of all, there is no point in blending teas with great character, for they will simply harm one another. Start with a neutral base, such as a China tea like Keemun, a South India tea (Nilgiri, Dooars, etc.), or even an African tea. These do not have an overwhelming personality yet will give the liquor a fine color. Then subtle notes may be added to this base—a little Lapsang Souchong for its smoky taste, or a hint of Darjeeling for its fruitiness, or even several grams of green tea to freshen and lighten the drink. Above all, however, it is important to know for what type of occasion and at what time of day the tea is to be served. As an example, the composition of two different types of classic blend are given below.

English Breakfast. A small-leaved tea generally composed of a Ceylon Broken Orange Pekoe with a hint of Assam or Darjeeling, or even another tea from South India or Africa. This very British blend is obviously drunk with a drop of milk and goes well with toast, honey and jam. It is not only ideal for breakfast, but can be enjoyed throughout the morning.

Five O'clock Tea. Another typically English blend, this time using whole-leaf Ceylon teas (O.P., F.O.P.). Somewhat full-bodied, the blend nevertheless gives a light, aromatic brew. Milk can be added, but the tea is delightful as is. An afternoon tea to be drunk on its own or with a snack of cakes and sweets.

SCENTED TEAS

The infatuation with scented teas that swept across France, Germany and Switzerland in the 1970s produced a veritable explosion of diverse—and sometimes bizarre—flavors that made purists shudder. So much so that it was often forgotten that this motley tribe of rhubarb, pistachio, coconut and chocolate teas descends from extremely refined Asian ancestors. Scented teas include a number of classics that are a delight to drink in the evening. Sugar may sometimes enhance their flavor, but milk is to be avoided.

Earl Grey. A China or Darjee-

36 · RUSSIAN O. P.

37 · FIVE O'CLOCK TEA

38 · EARL GREY

39 · JASMINE TEA

40 · ROSE TEA

ling tea (though green and semifermented teas are now sometimes used) scented with oil from the peel of bergamot, a Canton orange. Made fashionable by Earl Grey, the British prime minister, after a visit to China in 1830.

Jasmine or Rose Tea. The finest teas of this type come from China and are produced on the plantation itself, according to ancestral recipes. Freshly cut flowers are added to the tea so that it is impregnated with their aroma. Whether the flowers are subsequently removed or left in the tea makes little difference to the ultimate taste of the beverage, but nothing is more delightful than to find a few petals among the tea leaves.

Imperial Russian. Originally from China, but particularly appreciated by Russian high society in the nineteenth century, this tea is flavored with bergamot and other citrus scents.

Tea tasting was done in collaboration with Mariage Frères tea dealers in Paris.

TEA FOR GOURMETS

Westerners do not yet associate tea with gastronomy. People who frequent Chinese restaurants, of course, are used to the idea of savoring jasmine tea with exotic dishes. But such occasions provide only a faint glimmer of the infinite possibilities offered by tea. For it is entirely feasible to drink tea throughout a well-prepared Western-style meal, selecting the right tea with each course just as one would normally choose wines. Green or smoky tea goes well with fish, whereas Earl Grey, Darjeeling and Oolong are more appropriate with fowl. As to desserts, all the light, scented, large-leafed teas provide interesting options. There are, in fact, no precise rules—an adventurous palate and a little imagination are all that are required.

Furthermore, tea can be a delightful ingredient in gourmet recipes. The number of these recipes is limited because the subtle character of tea is easily overwhelmed by other, stronger flavors. Included below are nevertheless several delicate and refined combinations that are well worth trying.

E a r l   G r e y   S a u c e

Ingredients: 1 cup chicken stock (bouillon cubes can be used), 1 heaping tablespoon Earl Grey tea, 1/4 cup heavy cream, 2 teaspoons of sugar, several drops of lemon juice, salt and pepper.
Bring the chicken stock to a boil, then steep the tea in it for three minutes. Boil cream with sugar over high heat until reduced by half. Strain stock and add to cream.
Reduce heat to low and continue to reduce, beating vigorously to produce a frothy texture. Add lemon juice and season with salt and pepper to taste. This sauce delightfully accompanies fowl, notably duck.

M a t c h a   S a u c e

Ingredients: 2 cups fish stock, 1/4 cup heavy cream, 1/4 teaspoon powdered Matcha or green Japan tea (do not exceed this amount, as the taste is very strong), several drops of lemon juice, salt and pepper.
Boil stock over high heat until reduced by half. Add cream and continue boiling until thick enough to coat the back of a spoon. Reduce heat to low, add Matcha and lemon juice and beat until a thick, light sauce is obtained. Season to taste with salt and pepper. Matcha sauce is delicious with sea trout and salmon.

T e a   J e l l y

Ingredients: 1 quart of steeped tea, 6 to 8 cups sugar, 1/2 cup apple pectin, juice of 1 1/2 lemons.
Bring the tea to a boil. Add the sugar, pectin and lemon juice. Bring back to a boil and continue cooking for four minutes. Place in jars, cover with a piece of plastic wrap and let cool.

B l a c k   T e a   I c e   C r e a m

Ingredients for four servings: 1/2 liter of milk, 5 egg yolks, 1 1/4 cups sugar, 1 tablespoon tea from Uva Highlands (a famous Ceylon tea estate).
Bring half the milk to a boil. Meanwhile, add the sugar to the egg yolks, beating until the mixture becomes whitish. Add it little by little to the cold milk and set aside. Steep the tea in the hot milk for four minutes, strain the leaves, and beat the hot milk into the egg yolk mixture. Pour into a pan and cook over very low heat for five minutes, stirring continuously with a wooden spoon. Cool completely and freeze according to manufacturer's instructions in an ice cream maker.

T e a   G r a n i t a

Ingredients for eight servings: 1 cup Ceylon Orange Pekoe tea, 1 1/2 cups sugar, 2 tablespoons powdered milk, 1/4 cup white rum.
Steep the tea in 1 quart of boiling water for ten minutes. Strain the leaves and add 1 cup

This "Still-life with Tea" was photographed in the Mariage Frères tea salon. The foreground contains Mont Fuji, a creamy mousse made from green Japan tea, behind which can be seen a measure of powdered green Matcha Uji (in a spoon made from the bark of a cherry tree), a bowl of frothy tea, and the bamboo whisk used to whip the tea. On the left is a custard cream made with black tea, a bowl of tea jelly, a tea-scented candle, and a braid of tea to be plunged into a bathtub to perfume the water. The document concerns a shipment of tea imported by Mariage Frères in 1888.

of the sugar to the tea, stirring well. Pour into a glass or ceramic baking dish and place in the freezer.

When small patches of ice crystals appear on the surface, remove the dish from the freezer and transfer contents to a food processor. Add the powdered milk and process briefly to break up crystals. Return mixture to the freezer for ten minutes, then blend again. Repeat the operation about ten times until the mixture begins to resemble a cream. Add the rum and the remaining sugar. Blend one last time, return to the freezer briefly and serve immediately in individual bowls.

Green Tea Ice Cream

Ingredients for eight servings: 1 quart heavy cream, 2 cups milk, 1 1/4 cups sugar, a pinch of salt and 1/4 teaspoon green tea (preferably Matcha Uji).
Boil cream over high heat until reduced by half. Bring to room temperature, cover and refrigerate until well chilled.
Combine reduced cream with remaining ingredients and mix until sugar is dissolved. Pour into ice trays.

Mount Fuji

Ingredients for six servings: 1 cup milk, 1/2 cup powdered sugar, 6 egg yolks, 1 envelope gelatin, 1 scant teaspoon Matcha or green Japan tea, and 1 cup heavy cream.
Make a custard by blending the egg yolks and sugar until whitish. Heat the milk and the egg mixture, cooking over low heat and stirring continuously with a wooden spoon.
Sprinkle the gelatin over 1/4 cup cold water and let sit for five minutes to dissolve. When custard is creamy, take it off the heat and add the Matcha and the gelatin. It is important to let the mixture cool completely. Whip the cream and gently fold it into the cold custard.

Spoon into individual cups and place in the refrigerator for twenty-four hours.

Iced Tea

Iced tea is an outstandingly refreshing and invigorating drink, but should not be steeped in hot water, for it becomes cloudy and unattractive as it cools. Exceptionally clear iced tea can be obtained by steeping the tea in cold water and leaving it in the refrigerator for twelve hours.
The tea can then be drunk straight or on ice, or mixed with other ingredients to make cocktails.

Sakura Cocktail

Ingredients: Champagne, a simple sugar syrup made of equal amounts of sugar and water heated to dissolve then completely chilled, maraschino cherries and Sakura tea (12 cups tea for 1 quart of water).
Steep the tea in cold water. Add sugar syrup to taste. Chill champagne glasses, place a cherry in the bottom, then add 1/3 tea and 2/3 champagne.
Serve ice-cold.

Tea-Clipper Cocktail

Ingredients: Fresh apple juice, cinnamon tea (1/2 cup for 2 cups water), ice cubes.
Prepare cinnamon-flavored iced tea. Chill tall cocktail glasses. To serve, place ice cubes in the bottom of each glass and pour in 1/3 tea and 2/3 apple juice. Decorate with a slice of lime and serve ice cold.

The above recipes were provided by Mariage Frères, Paris, except for the Tea Granita and the iced tea drinks.

A CONNOISSEUR'S GUIDE

French author Jean-Paul Aron, in a preface to a book on chocolate, claimed that "tea evokes the calm of bedrooms, the warmth of Russian isbas, the reserve of English gentlemen... The island-dwelling British are not the only Europeans to be keen on tea, for continentals consigned to wintry conviviality also appreciate it." Excellent tea is now served on both sides of the English Channel, and the affirmation by Charles Laughton in Leo McCarey's 1935 film *Ruggles of Red Gap* that tea is "an English affair" is now something of a cliché. For it has also become "an international affair," as this guide to fine establishments in the United States, London and Paris shows, demonstrating that it is becoming easier to taste and buy high-quality tea and tea accessories.

T E A
R O O M S

NEW YORK

THE ALGONQUIN
59 West 44th Street, New York,
NY 10036
Tel.: 212 840-6400 or 888 304-2047
www.algonquinhotel.com
Famous for its literary days of the Round Table, this charming hotel in the middle of the theater district offers a wide array of teas. Pastries, English muffins, cinnamon toast, scones with Devonshire clotted cream as well as savory items like cheese with crackers and finger sandwiches are available every afternoon from 4:00 to 5:00.

THE BOOK-FRIENDS CAFÉ
16 West 18th Street, New York,
NY 10011. Tel.: 212 255-7407
Actually a bookshop, this informal setting provides a comfortable place to browse while sipping tea selected from an interesting and varied menu. Tea sandwiches, scones and cakes are offered every afternoon from 3:00 to 5:00. The bookshop carries several good books devoted to tea and tea consumption.

MARK'S
The Mark Hotel, 25 East 77th Street,
New York, NY 10021.
Tel.: 212 744-4300
www.themarkhotel.com
High tea is served daily in this elegant Upper East Side gem of a restaurant. Flawless service and excellent pastries make this a real "must-do" for tea aficionados.

THE PALM COURT
The Plaza Hotel, 768 Fifth Avenue,
New York, NY 10019
Tel.: 212 759-3000
People come from all over the country to enjoy the elegant English tea at the Plaza. From 3:45 to 6:00 Monday through Saturday (4:00 to 6:00 on Sunday), tea-lovers can choose from fifteen varieties as well as scones, tiny sandwiches, miniature pastries and a full à la carte menu. Tea in this most regal of settings comes complete with chamber music and excellent service.

THE ROTUNDA
The Hotel Pierre, 795 Fifth Avenue,
New York, NY 10021.
Tel.: 212 838-8000
Tea is served in the beautiful Rotunda, an oval room with walls displaying a handsome mural. Elegant surroundings and impeccable service make the Pierre one of the best places in town to sample a carefully selected choice of fine teas as well as thin sandwiches, sumptuous pastries and scones.

THE STANHOPE
995 Fifth Avenue, New York,
NY 10028. Tel.: 212 774-1234
www.stanhopepark.hyatt.com
Traditional tea is served every afternoon in the comfortable, intimate surroundings of this charming hotel, which is located right across the street from the Metropolitan Museum.

CHICAGO

THE CONSERVATORY
Chicago Four Seasons Hotel, 120 East Delaware, Chicago, IL 60611-1428
Tel.: 312 280-8800
www.fourseasons.com/chicagofs
Located in the 900 North Michigan

Building, the Conservatory is in the lounge area of the seventh-floor lobby overlooking Michigan Avenue. Monday through Friday, a full tea and a light tea are available from 3:00 to 5:00; Saturday from 3:30 to 5:00. A selection of loose-leaf teas is served along with pastries and scones. A piano player is a popular feature here.

THE PALM COURT
The Drake Hotel, 140 East Walton Place, Chicago, IL 60611
Tel.: 312 787-2200
or 800 55DRAKE
www.thedrakehotel.com
A seventeenth-century bronze urn and a beautiful fountain make a wonderful setting for a traditional afternoon tea. This historical landmark has become a Chicago institution, dating back to the 1920s. Comfortable sofas, lush green plants and dark paneling provide a relaxing, warm atmosphere for enjoying specialties like currant buns, scones and muffins served with whipped cream and homemade strawberry preserves. A harpist provides music every afternoon from 3:00 to 5:30.

SAN FRANCISCO

CAMPTON PLACE
Campton Place Hotel, 340 Stockton Street, San Francisco, CA 94108
Tel.: 415 781-5555 or 800 235-4300
www.camptonplace.com
The cozy lounge area serves tea daily from 2:30 to 4:30. Individual pots of tea are served in beautiful silver sets with a choice of pastries and sandwiches. A balanced selection of imported teas are all first-rate. Comfortable chairs and a suitable low-key setting make Campton Place the perfect place for sipping and chatting.

LOS ANGELES

RENDEZVOUS COURT
The Biltmore Hotel, 506 Grand
Avenue, Los Angeles, CA 90071
Tel.: 213 624-1011
Located in the hotel's former lobby, the
cathedral-like, Spanish-Italian design
provides a regal yet comfortable stage
for tea. Stone columns, a carved two-
story vaulted ceiling and a magnificent
ornamental staircase combine to create a restful oasis after a busy day in
Los Angeles. The Biltmore features a
line of fine loose-leaf and herbal teas.
A simple Rendezvous Tea entails a pot
of tea and almond cookies. For the
Traditional Tea, a tiered silver tea caddy
is presented to the table fully laden
with canapés, sandwiches and pastries.

WASHINGTON D.C.

THE JEFFERSON
The Jefferson Hotel, 1200 16th Street
N.W., Washington, D.C. 20036
Tel.: 202 347-2000
www.loewhotels.com/hotels/
washington_jefferson
Afternoon tea here is quiet and quaint.
The library-like setting is peaceful and
soul-soothing, as is the constant glow of
the fire. Traditional service includes
cookies and strawberries, smoked-duck
sandwiches and an array of teas from all
corners of the world.

LONDON

BROWN'S HOTEL
Albemarle Street, Mayfair, London
W1S 4BP. Tel.: 020 7493-9381
www.brownshotel.com
Located just two minutes away from
Hyde Park, Brown's is well known for
its afternoon tea. Since tables cannot be
reserved, customers begin lining up at
three o'clock to make sure of obtaining
one of the flowery chintz armchairs
in the dark-paneled salon. Popular
varieties include Darjeeling, Keemun,
Gunpowder and Brown's Blend, accompanied by clotted cream, sandwiches,
toast or cakes.

CLARIDGE'S
Brook Street, Mayfair, London
W1A 2JQ. Tel.: 020 7629-8860

www.the-savoy-group.com/claridges
Tea can be taken in the "Reading
Room," whose 1925 decor alone is
worth the visit. Reservations are recommended.

MAIDS OF HONOUR
288 Kew Road, Kew Gardens,
Richmond, Surrey TW9 3DU
Tel.: 020 8940-2752
One of the oldest tea rooms in Great
Britain, and therefore a must for all tea-
lovers and historians.

PATISSERIE VALERIE AT SAGNE
105 Marylebone High Street, London
W1U 4RS. Tel.: 020 7395-6240
www.patisserie-valerie.co.uk
A tea and pastry shop with a 1920s
Pompeian decor right in the heart of
the Marylebone district. The somewhat continental-style tea is served
with excellent strawberry pies, walnut,
chocolate or praline pastries, crois-
sants or buns.

RITZ HOTEL
150 Piccadilly, London W1J 9BR
Tel.: 020 7493-8181
www.theritzhotel.co.uk
Tea is served in the Palm Court's superb nineteenth-century setting. The
elegance of Ritz service is notorious,
thanks to the variety of finger sandwiches made of cucumber, salmon, turkey, etc. Scones are accompanied by
strawberry jam and clotted cream.
Reservations are required if one is not
staying at the hotel.

SAVOY HOTEL
The Strand, London WC2R 0EU
Tel.: 020 7836-4343
www.savoy-group.co.uk
Tea at the Savoy is a grand London tradition. The well-trained and friendly
staff place teapots and cakes on rattan
tables in a room decorated with a trompe
l'œil fresco, overlooking the Thames.

WALDORF HOTEL
Aldwych, London WC2B 4DD
Tel.: 020 7836-2400
www.hilton.co.uk/Waldorf
The British tradition of tea dances is
still alive in the indoor garden of the
Palm Court Lounge with its palm trees
and orchestra. Between two waltzes,

dancers enjoy Earl Grey, Darjeeling,
Lapsang Souchong or a special blend
accompanied by cakes and sandwiches.

TEA TIME
21 The Pavement, Clapham, London
SW4 0HY. Tel.: 020 7622-0904
This fashionable tea room was founded
by Jane Pettigrew, author of *Tea Time*.
The many varieties of tea are accompanied by cakes and pastries made
following the original recipes found in
Pettigrew's book.

PARIS

ANGELINA
226 Rue de Rivoli, 75001 Paris
Tel.: 01 42 60 82 00
Palais des Congrès (Level 3),
24 Boulevard. Pershing, 75017 Paris
Tel.: 01 40 68 22 51
Galeries Lafayette Department
Store (Third Floor), 40 Boulevard
Haussmann, 75009 Paris
Tel.: 01 42 82 30 32
www.angelina.fr
The original salon on the Rue de Rivoli
has now been listed as being of histori-
cal interest, and the tea (including
Darjeeling and Lapsang Souchong) is
served in silver teapots. The Darjeeling
is particularly special because it is cul-
tivated in Angelina's own "garden."
Patrons may also buy Angelina's eleven
varieties of tea in the adjoining shop.

À PRIORI THÉ
35–37 Galerie Vivienne, 75002 Paris
Tel.: 01 42 97 48 75
In a large, quiet room decorated in
tones of beige, under a skylight,
habitués of A Priori Thé sample one of
the tea room's sixteen classic or scented
blends. This is one of the few Paris
salons to offer mint tea.

LA CHARLOTTE DE L'ISLE
14 Rue Saint-Louis-en-l'Isle,
75004 Paris. Tel.: 01 43 54 25 83
The tea menu is a real treasure trove,
with thirty-two tea varieties. Whether
you choose a classical brew or a less
conventional one, the tea will be served
in a Japanese cast-iron teapot.

LA COUR DE ROHAN
59–61 Rue Saint-André-des-Arts,
75005 Paris. Tel.: 01 43 25 79 67

Known for its elegant and luxurious charm, this plush salon teas offers eighteen teas, one of which is a Cour de Rohan blend produced by the owner himself. All teas are served in antique porcelain, and on Saturday nights the tea room is open late.

LADURÉE
16 Rue Royale, 75008 Paris
Tel.: 01 42 60 21 79
75 Avenue des Champs-Élysées,
75008 Paris. Tel.: 01 40 75 08 75
www.laduree.fr
This attractive tea room with its painted ceilings typical of the nineteenth century is known for its macaroons that go delightfully well with one of the three straightforward teas from Betjeman and Barton.

LES ENFANTS GÂTÉS
43 Rue des Francs-Bourgeois,
75004 Paris.
Tel.: 01 42 77 07 63
This combination art gallery and English club makes for a comfortable atmosphere. The menu provides clear and interesting explanations. A high-grown Darjeeling, a Keemun or an imaginatively scented tea is perfect for a delightful brunch or afternoon tea break.

INTERCONTINENTAL HOTEL
3 Rue de Castiglione, 75001 Paris
Tel.: 01 47 77 11 11
www.paris-ic.intercontinental.com
Real English tea can be had in the Lobby Bar—to the strains of a harp—or on the terrace. A good selection of seven teas is served in Wedgwood china, accompanied by English muffins, scones, cakes, cucumber sandwiches and Devonshire clotted cream.

LE LOIR DANS LA THÉIERE
3 Rue des Rosiers, 75004 Paris
Tel.: 01 42 72 90 61
Settle into an armchair or sofa and while away the time over a cup of one of the thirty-seven teas on the menu (including many scented varieties), admiring the old cupboards and a fresco of Alice in Wonderland.

MARIAGE FRÈRES
30–32 Rue du Bourg-Tibourg,
75004 Paris

Tel.: 01 42 72 28 11
13 Rue des Grands-Augustins,
75006 Paris
Tel.: 01 40 51 82 50
260 Rue du Faubourg-St-Honoré,
75008 Paris
Tel.: 01 46 22 18 54
www.mariagefreres.com
Tea rooms have been opened alongside the age-old tea counters at each of the famous Mariage outlets. The skylit Bourg-Tibourg salon evokes the warm colonial climate and, behind the bar a specialist prepares and tastes each tea. If you don't know what to order, one of the white garbed waiters will skillfully guide you through the list of three hundred and fifty teas (plus special additions depending on availability). This is the place to be seduced by a white tea from Fujian (for true connoisseurs only), by tea jellies, or by the trolley of delicious pies and tea-flavored desserts. Over on Rue des Grands Augustins, in a seventeenth-century residence officially listed as a historical site, tea is taken either in a vaulted cellar evoking the "tea docks" from colonial days, or on an upper floor bedecked with tall, elegant windows. Sunday brunch is highly fashionable at both establishments.

LE MEURICE
228 Rue de Rivoli, 75001 Paris
Tel.: 01 44 58 10 10
www.meuricehotel.com
In the very fine setting of its Pompadour Salon, the Meurice Hotel offers fifteen varieties of tea, including classic and scented blends. All are served in silver teapots, accompanied by toast, cakes or petit fours.

MOSQUE
19 Rue Geoffroy-Saint-Hilaire,
75005 Paris. Tel.: 01 43 31 18 14
The Paris Mosque's café is the only place in town where traditional North African mint tea can be savored in a superbly Moorish interior (winter) or on a cool patio (summer).

LE PLAZA ATHENÉE
21 Avenue Montaigne, 75008 Paris
Tel.: 01 53 67 66 65
The hotel's Gobelins Gallery proposes a selection of four teas, to be savored to the sound of a piano. Meanwhile,

the Relais Plaza restaurant (a reconstitution of the dining room on the cruise ship *Normandie*) offers a full English tea to the strains of a harp. Toasted buns, scones, tiny sandwiches and cream accompany one of twenty-three teas, including the Plaza's Secret Blend.

HOTEL RITZ
15 Place Vendôme, 75001 Paris
Tel.: 01 43 16 30 30. www.ritzparis.com
Every day at four o'clock, afternoon tea can be had at the Vendôme bar. Sit back in a plush sofa in winter, or enjoy the fine terrace in summer. Twelve teas, including a good green tea and a theine-free variety, are served along with sandwiches, petit fours and hot muffins.

TEA CADDY
14 Rue Saint-Julien-le-Pauvre,
75005 Paris. Tel.: 01 43 54 15 56
Located opposite a charming little church, this very British tea room has remained unchanged since it was founded in 1928 by a Miss Kinklin. The last generals of the Indian Army often met there to reminisce. Nostalgia comes in the form of a dozen teas, including Imperial Russian, Lapsang Souchong, Assam and Darjeeling, accompanied by delicious homemade cakes.

THE COOL
10 Rue Saint-Florentin, 75001 Paris
Tel.: 01 42 24 69 13
Paintings are exhibited in this tea room that features a fine selection of 25 teas, all served in Japanese iron-cast teapots. For breakfast, lunch or tea.

TORAYA
10 Rue Saint-Florentin, 75001 Paris
Tel.: 01 42 60 13 00
www.toraya-group.co.jp
Purveyors to His Majesty the Emperor of Japan for four hundred years, the Toraya firm has recently opened a salon in Paris decorated in black lacquer and bamboo. It offers two green teas—a Sencha and a Matcha—prepared strictly according to traditional rules and accompanied by a *zangetsu* or other sweet made from *adzuki* beans. Both teas are imported directly from Japan and are also sold in a shop next to the tea room.

T E A
S H O P S

NEW YORK

BLOOMINGDALES
100 Third Avenue, New York,
NY 10022. Tel.: 212 705-2000
www.bloomingdales.com
Highly select teas are sold in the food department of this most famous of department stores. Exotic teas like Ceylorese Berubeul, Indian Travancore Highgrown and Japanese Sencha grace the shelves. Bloomingdales has just introduced the exclusive Mariage Frères teas from Paris, an American first.

MCNULTY'S TEA AND COFFEE COMPANY
109 Christopher Street, New York,
NY 10014. Tel.: 212 242-5351
www.mcnultys.com
A Greenwich Village institution, McNulty's offers some of the best teas available in New York. Earl Grey, English Breakfast and Darjeeling are among the favorites. Japan teas sold here are Bancha, Japan Green Pan-Fired brands, and China teas include Gunpowder, Young Hyson and Lung Ching. The toll-free number for mailing and shipping is: 800 356-5200.

PORTO RICO
201 Bleeker Street, New York,
NY 10012. Tel.: 212 GR7-5421
www.portorico.com
People line up to buy teas from all over the world at this New York landmark. Darjeeling, Assam and an assortment of green teas are among the 100 varieties available. The toll-free order and shipping number is: 800 453-5908.

LONDON

FORTNUM AND MASON
181 Piccadilly, London W1V 0BB
Tel.: 020 734-8040
www.fortnumandmason.com
Fortnum and Mason is a veritable institution, having been suppliers to the British aristocracy for nearly three hundred years. The elegant and ever-popular tea department offers forty varieties in green or red tins, including Darjeeling, Assam, Ceylon, Formosa and China teas as well as the famous blends named Royal, Crown, Celebration, Breakfast, Fortmason, New York, Queen Anne. Several Fortnum and Mason teas may also be sampled on the premises.

HARRODS
Brompton Road, Knightsbridge,
London SW1 7XL
www.harrods.com
In the amazing setting of Harrod's famous "Food Hall", the tea department sells Betjeman and Barton teas. Prince Charles reportedly prefers the Pushkin blend with its aroma of bergamot and other citrus flavors.

TEA HOUSE
15a Neal Street, Covent Garden,
London WC2 H9PU.
Tel.: 020 7240-7539
This unusual shop with its red-and-black brick façade offers forty-five varieties of tea from India, China and Japan, as well as a full range of "Teaphernalia," tea-related products and utensils. Tea may be ordered by mail. Tea House outlets are also located in Oxford and Stratford-upon-Avon.

TWININGS
216 The Strand, London WC2 1AP
Tel.: 020 7353-3511
www.twinings.com
Founded in 1706 by Thomas Twining, this is the oldest tea shop in London. It offers a selection of over fifty teas, and houses a small museum displaying the biggest teapot in the world.

WHITTARD & CO., LTD.
For information on shop locations,
call 0800 015-4394 (UK only)
or 020 7819-6510.
www.whittard.co.uk
One of London's oldest tea merchants, Whittard & Company import directly from China, Japan, Ceylon and Formosa. Their popular varieties include Mango Indica, Spice Imperial and first flush Darjeelings.

PARIS

BETJEMAN AND BARTON
23 Boulevard Malesherbes,
75008 Paris. Tel.: 01 42 65 86 17
24 Boulevard des Filles-du-Calvaire,
75003 Paris. Tel.: 01 40 21 35 52
www.betjemanandbarton.com
This shop is regularly visited by tea-lovers. Every day, a cup of one of the hundred and twenty teas stored in either red or green canisters (and fully described in Betjeman and Barton's catalog) is offered to customers—with any luck you may drop in when a Saint James Fannings or a Castleton G.F.O.P. second flush is being brewed. The store also sells teapots, strainers, infusers, whisks for Matcha, metallic and lacquer containers, and fine wooden tea caddies, not to mention B & B's exclusive nylon teabags that preserve the full flavor of the four teas thus packaged. Furthermore, customers will find scones, crumpets, English muffins, mince pies and tea jellies. The firm is headed by Didier Jumeau-Lafond, a renowned tea connoisseur. Betjeman and Barton was founded in Paris in 1919, and now exports to Japan, Australia, the United States, and elsewhere. For a modest fee you can purchase their well-produced catalog known as "the little book of tea."

COMPAGNIE ANGLAISE DES THÉS
60 Rue du Cherche-Midi, 75006 Paris
Tel.: 01 45 49 45 96
Founded in 1823, and once official purveyor to Napoleon III, this tiny shop is just a stones throw from the Champs-Elysées. The wood-paneled interior houses a hundred varieties of tea, including fine Darjeelings, a China Paklum, and the famous Lotus Flower Tea. One Darjeeling comes in muslin teabags, and the store sells a range of imaginative teapots. Personal blends can also be ordered on Rue Lecourbe and at the Forum des Halles.

LES CONTES DE THÉ
60 Rue du Cherche-Midi, 75006 Paris
Tel.: 01 45 49 45 96
In addition to a good selection of Ceylon, Assam, Darjeeling and China teas, this boutique stocks teas from Brazil and Mauritius. The eighty-five varieties also include an unusual green Japan

Hojicha, a grilled tea of light and incomparable flavor, to be drunk with meals. A wide range of scented teas from England are sold in teabag form. Three hundred and fifty teapots, many of eccentric design, are also on sale along with tea caddies, samovars and tea cozies.

ESTRELLA
34 Rue Saint-Sulpice, 75006 Paris
Tel.: 01 46 33 16 37
This little shop sells one hundred and twenty teas in bulk, a number of which also come in 125 gram (3 1/2 oz.) packets. Estrella creates its own aromatic blends and stocks a dozen different Darjeelings, as well as a selection of teas from Fortnum and Mason and Jackson's of Piccadilly.

FAUCHON
26 Place de la Madeleine, 75008 Paris
Tel.: 01 47 42 60 11. www.fauchon.com
This prestigious Paris catering firm was founded over a century ago, and includes a tea department that sells sixty varieties of tea in bulk, including excellent high-grown harvests, exclusive blends, and scented teas. Fans of Darjeeling will appreciate the Jungpana, with its delicious aroma of ripe peaches, or may sample the Kee-Yu, an unusual and especially smooth blend of China teas. Every day a different cup of tea is offered to customers for tasting.

GALERIES LAFAYETTE
40 Boulevard Haussmann, 75009 Paris
Tel.: 01 42 82 34 56
www.galerieslafayette.com
The "gourmet" boutique in this vast department store sells forty varieties of tea, notably a range of Asian teas, including six Darjeelings, a Formosa Gunpowder, and three green Japan teas as well as many scented teas. A cup of tea may be sampled at the counter.

HÉDIARD
21 Place de la Madeleine, 75008 Paris
Tel.: 01 43 12 88 88. www.hediard.fr

In a small red shop just off the square, a knowledgeable sales-woman can suggest one of Hédiard's one hundred teas, including twenty-eight classic varieties, three theinefree teas, and seventy scented blends. The famous Hédiard Blend sits alongside a superb range of outstanding Darjeelings such as the ever-so-subtle Puttabong. Hédiard also carries a selection of teabags, packaged mint tea, and a few Fortnum and Mason blends.

MARIAGE FRÈRES
30–32 Rue du Bourg-Tibourg,
75004 Paris. Tel.: 01 42 72 28 11
13 Rue des Grands-Augustins,
75006 Paris. Tel.: 01 40 51 82 50
260 Rue du Faubourg-St-Honoré,
75008 Paris. Tel.: 01 46 22 18 54
www.mariagefreres.com
On entering either of these enticing shops, customers feel as though they have walked onto a movie set or back into the past. Near a colonial-style counter, between chests of tea from China, are displayed canisters of over three hundred and fifty types of tea. The tricky task of choosing one is facilitated by the purchase of a small catalog and by the competent sales staff who can guide you through the thirty tea-producing countries, the exclusive blends and the amazing Darjeelings such as Puttabong and Upper Namring. Over three hundred tea services, old and new, are sold alongside samovars, infusers, rock sugar, containers in metal or cherry bark, and even tea-scented candles. There are also four types of jelly and sweets made from tea and five varieties of chocolate with tea-flavored fillings. There are even braided mats of tea to be plunged into the bathtub to perfume the water. There is obviously a wide range of teapots on sale, whether cast-iron, porcelain, ceramic, or silver-plated (including the 1930 model used in the tea room, which keeps the tea at the right temperature). Finally, customers may

wish to buy a reproduction of a seventeenth-century English tea caddy made of precious wood. Mariage Frères has now opened a Tea Museum in the Rue du Bourg-Tibourg outlet, where rare objects from the eighteenth and nineteenth century are displayed.

LE PALAIS DES THÉS
35 Rue de l'Abbé-Grégoire,
75006 Paris. Tel.: 01 45 48 85 81
21 Rue Raymond-Losserand, 75014
Paris. Tel.: 01 43 21 97 97
www.palaisdesthes.com
Three hundred types of tea are displayed in canisters, each one listed in the "tea-lover's handbook." The shop also sells old and new samovars, teapots, and all the utensils needed for the tea ritual. There is also a complete tea-lover's library that shows a marked penchant for Russian teas. You can try out your samovar with teas from Georgia, Azerbaijan, and the Caucasus, as well as nine Russian Imperial blends. Le Palais des Thés also proposes its famous Monks' Tea and the Compagnie Coloniale brand of muslin teabags. The store accepts mail orders.

TORRECFACTION GUIRAUD
21 Boulevard de Reuilly, 75012 Paris
Tel.: 01 43 43 39 27
One hundred and two teas are available here: smoked, perfumed, green, or black, as well as a large range of teas from China (Ching Wo, Congou, Caravane), the gardens of Assam (Keylung, Napuk) and Darjeeling (Jungpana, Bloomfield).

VERLET
246 Rue Saint-Honoré, 75001 Paris
Tel.: 01 42 60 67 39
Verlet is a skilful artisan trader, well respected for his talent. Better known for his coffees, he also has about thirty carefully selected teas amongst his wares. While on-spot-tastings are possible, the coffee aromas are too strong to do the teas justice.

GLOSSARY

ASSAM: A region in northeastern India known for its strong, high-grade tea.

AUTUMNAL: India and Formosa teas harvested in autumn, and therefore touched with cool weather.

BASKET-FIRED: Japan tea that has been cured in baskets by firing.

BLACK TEA: Tea that has been withered, rolled (or macerated), fermented, fired (or dried), and sorted into grades.

BLENDER: A taster who decides on the proportions of each variety required to produce the flavor of a given blend.

BRICK TEA: Common grades of China and Japan teas, mixed with stalk and dust, molded into bricks under high pressure.

BROKEN ORANGE PEKOE (B.O.P.): Black tea comprising smaller leaves and broken segments with some tips, harvested by the fine plucking method. When an abundance of tips is included, the grade becomes F.B.O.P. (Flowery Broken Orange Pekoe).

BROKEN PEKOE (B.P.): Full-bodied black tea comprising broken segments of somewhat coarse leaves, without tips.

CACHAR: The most common variety of India tea from the Cachar district of Assam.

CAMELLIA SINENSIS: Botanical name for the tea plant.

CEYLON: Former name of Sri Lanka, still occasionally used when referring to tea grown on the island.

CHING WO: Black China tea from Fujian province.

CHUNMEE: Green China tea, so called due to its resemblance to the shape of human eyebrows.

CONGOU: A general term used to describe all black teas from China.

C.T.C.: Crushing/Tearing/Curling. A mechanized method of macerating tea (as opposed to rolling) that speeds fermentation of black teas and accelerates production time.

DARJEELING: A province in northern India that produces black tea famous for its exquisite bouquet.

DIMBULA: A district in Sri Lanka that produces full-bodied black tea.

DOOARS: A district in northern India that produces a black tea of the same name.

DUST: Black tea in small siftings of less than a millimeter, practically reduced to powder.

EARL GREY: A black China tea scented with oil of bergamot.

ENGLISH BREAKFAST: A name originally applied to China Congou in the United States, and now used to include blends of black teas in which the China flavor predominates.

ESTATE: A property or holding that may include more than one garden under the same management or ownership.

FANNINGS: Small grainy particles of leaf (1 to 1.5 mm) sifted out of the better-grade teas. They produce a liquor that is often as good as that of whole leaf grades.

FERMENTATION: A stage in the production of black tea involving oxidation of enzymes naturally found in the tea leaf.

FLOWERY ORANGE PEKOE: Orange Pekoe with an abundance of tips, and therefore of finer quality.

FLOWERY PEKOE: Whole-leaf black tea with the leaves rolled lengthwise.

FLUSH: Young tea leaf shoots. The term also refers to the various harvests—thus "first flush" is the early, spring plucking whereas "second flush" is harvested in late spring and early summer.

FORMOSA: The island known as Taiwan. Produces Oolong, Pouchong and black teas.

GARDEN: The name of a specific plantation, used to identify harvests produced solely from that garden. In Ceylon, gardens are sometimes referred to as "estates."

GOLDEN TIPS: Orange-colored buds found in certain black teas.

GOVERNMENT STANDARDS: Grades of teas selected annually as import standards of purity, quality and fitness for consumption by the U.S. Board of Tea Experts.

GREEN TEA: Unfermented tea that is immediately heated (or steamed) to kill the fermentation enzymes. Then it is rolled and dried.

GUNPOWDER: A type of young green tea, each leaf is rolled into a ball.

GYOKURO: Japanese for "pearl dew." A high-grade tea made by a special process in the Uji district of Japan, using tea grown on shaded bushes.

HIGH TEA: An afternoon or evening meal with meat and other dishes at which tea is the main beverage.

HYSON: Chinese for "flourishing spring." A type of green China tea, formerly drunk extensively in Europe. "Young Hyson" is a type of China tea plucked early.

KEEMUN (or KEEMUM): A fine grade of black-leaf China Congou tea produced in Anliui province.

LAPSANG SOUCHONG: A smoky China tea.

LEGG CUT: A mechanized method for cutting leaves prior to fermentation and firing. Eliminates the withering stage and produces Fannings and Dust grade teas.

MATCHA: Powdered green tea from Japan, used in the tea ceremony.

NATURAL LEAF: Whole-leaf green tea from Japan, similar to "panfired" but with less rolling, also known as "porcelain-fired."

NILGIRI: A district in the hills of southern India that produces black tea.

OOLONG: Semi-fermented tea from China or Formosa.

ORANGE PEKOE (O.P.): Black tea comprising leaves 8 to 15 millimeters long. It has fewer tips than F.O.P. because it is plucked somewhat later in the season.

PAN-FIRED: A kind of Japan tea that is steamed, then rolled in iron pans over charcoal fires.

PEKOE: A grade of black tea produced by a medium plucking of the second leaf on the bush.

PEKOE SOUCHONG: Black tea, each leaf of which is rolled in a ball, produced by a coarse plucking of the third leaf on the bush.

POUCHONG: A kind of scented China tea, so called from the Cantonese method of packing in small paper packets, each of which was supposed to be the produce of one choice tea plant.

ROLLING: A stage in manufacture designed to break down the cell walls of the tea leaf so that it releases its essential oils.

SCENTED TEA: Green, semi-fermented or black tea that has been flavored by the addition of flowers, fruit or essential oils. Earl Grey is one of the most famous of scented teas.

SEMI-FERMENTED TEA: Tea that has been partially fermented, lending it qualities halfway between green and black tea.

SENCHA: The most popular variety of green tea in Japan.

SMOKY TEA: Black tea from China or Formosa that has been smoked over a wood fire.

SORTING: A stage in manufacturing in which the leaves are sifted, or sorted, into different sizes and grades.

SPRING TEAS: Formosa teas picked in the April-May season.

SUMMER TEAS: Formosa teas picked in the June-September season.

SZECHWAN: A non-smoky black tea from China, with narrow leaves and flowery fragrance.

TANNIN: An astringent chemical constituent of tea.
TARRY SOUCHONG: Very smoky black tea from China or Formosa.
TEA CADDY: A small container (often with lock and key) for tea, from *catty*, the Chinese and/or Malayan word for "pound," the quantity of tea originally contained in a caddy.

TEA TASTER: An expert judge of leaf and cup quality at all stages of production, brokerage, and final packaging.
THEINE: Another name for the caffeine contained in tea.
TIP: The bud leaf on a tea plant.
TIPPY TEAS: Teas with white or golden tips.
UVA: A district in Ceylon (Sri Lanka)

that produces a tea of great subtlety.
WITHERING: The initial stage in the manufacture of black tea, designed to reduce moisture content in the leaves so that they can be rolled or macerated.
YUNNAN: Black tea from the Yunnan province of China. Along with Assam, this region was the original site of wild tea plants.

INDEX

PHOTOGRAPHIC CREDITS

Copyediting: Julie Gaskill
Typesetting: Éditions de l'Après-Midi
Research: Fui Lee Luk
Color Separation: Colourscan France
Distributed in North America by Rizzoli International Publications, Inc.

Originally published in French as
Le Livre du Thé © Flammarion, 1991

English-language edition first published in 1992
ISBN: 2-0801-3533-3 © Flammarion

This edition © Éditions Flammarion, 2005

04 05 06 4 3 2 1

FC0478-05-I
ISBN: 2-0803-0478-X
Dépôt légal: 01/2005

Printed in Italy by Canale

可以吃，哪些有毒不能吃。這樣，他就開始試嚐百草。當他嚐到這種綠色花朵的樹上的嫩葉，一到肚子裡，就從下到上，從上到下，到處流動洗滌，好似把腸胃洗滌得乾乾淨淨，他就把腸胃洗滌的「查」叫做「茶」了。

神農嚐這種綠葉為「查」，以後人們喚百草，每天得中毒幾次，全靠茶來解救。茶和其他植物一樣，從發現到利用，需要經過一段漫長的過程。當原始人類發現茶葉對人體有醫療效用以後，對茶葉最初只作藥用；到了春秋時代，已提到用茶葉作菜飲，但沒有作茶飲的記載。

對茶葉作飲料的時間，前後相距竟有一千多年之久。其實，我國飲茶開始的年代，無論說是秦漢或是春秋，都說得太遲，更不消說是在晉代了。根據記載，周武王伐紂後，巴蜀等地曾以所產的茶葉作貢品。我國西南一帶的茶葉作飲料相當普遍了。在西晉以前，中國廣大地區還是把茶葉作為一種比較珍貴的飲料。

到了兩晉、南北朝，產茶漸多，傳播日廣，關於飲茶的記載也日益增多。據《晉書》記載，敦煌人單道開是西晉末年的僧徒，他在鄴都（今河南安陽）坐禪，不畏寒暑，晝夜不臥，每日吞服幾粒小石子一樣的丸藥，「大如梧子，藥有松蜜姜桂茯苓之氣」，似乎是蒙古人現在還通用的固形牛奶，混合以松子、桂皮、蜂蜜、姜、茯苓等而成的。此外，只《中興書》有一段是吳興太守陸納生活儉朴，以茶果待客老代，飲茶蘇（又稱茶粥）二升。《廣陵耆老傳》中提到：「晉元帝時，有老姥每旦獨提一器茗，往市鬻之，市人竟買。」

茶葉作為珍貴的貢品，由此可以推想到西周以前，即開始招收學童，傳授生產茶葉的技藝。沒有人民群眾對茶樹的栽培和製茶經驗，哪裡能夠「課童採茗」呢？可以想見，我國江南一帶，早在漢代，飲茶就相當盛行了。

在晉以後，我國江蘇、浙江一帶的茶葉作為飲料，哪裡能夠「課童藝茶」！漢代，曾在宴會上密賜茶名代酒，於是有人認為產茶飲之事，即產茶和飲之事，也有根據晉司馬相如《凡將篇》說「蔎」即是茶。有一根據晉張載《登成都樓詩》「芳荼冠六清，溢味播九區」之句，有人根據西漢揚雄《蜀都賦》中說的「百草兮，翠紫青黃」，沿長江逐漸向中、下游推進，傳播，這是陝西、河南等地成為北方古老茶區的原因。同時，傳播時發展成為日常飲料，有許多文獻的記載。有的人認為「秦人取蜀」（四川），而作者說茶，眾說紛紜。

左右奉帝，后向日侍帝不謹，不合啜此茶。」反映在西漢時期，茶已成為皇室中的一種飲料了。又據史料記載，漢王曾在江蘇宜興茗嶺「課童藝茶」；浙江臨海海雲賁竹山有仙翁茶園，漢朝名士江余姚人虞洪，上山採茗，遇仙人丹丘子，獲得大茗，等等。說明當時在江蘇、浙江一帶，已有茶樹栽植，並且往年已納入常生活中不可缺少的必需品。

唐朝李肇著的《國史補》記載：唐朝有使者叫常魯公，到了西番，烹茶帳中，有人拿出來指著所謂茶。」據說，我這裡也有，於是叫人拿出來指著說：「此壽州者、此舒州者、此顧渚者、此蘄門者、此昌明者、此邕湖者。」可見唐時飲茶風氣之盛，連新疆、西藏一帶的王公貴族家裡都已貯備各色名茶了。吐蕃的松贊干布贊普有兩個王妃，一是尼泊爾輸入西藏，文化與飲茶的風尚從內地輸入西藏從此飲茶與佛教更進一步結合，導致以後在西藏喇嘛寺中盛大茶會的出現。唐代茶葉已成為全國人民主要的消費品，茶區域已很遼闊，湖北、四川、雲南、廣西、貴州、河南等地，產茶較多。浮梁、湖州都是著名的茶產地基本相同。當以《白居易《琵琶行》中有「商人重利輕別離，前月浮梁買茶去」之句。唐德宗貞元九年（公元七九三年），茶稅也開始徵收了。到了宋代，茶已發展為交換西北邊區土特產的主要商品，清代，飲茶風氣愈盛。到元、明、清代，飲茶風氣愈盛。

文人學士提倡茗飲，紛紛以茶作為吟詩作賦的題材。最初提到我國茶葉的是明世宗嘉靖三十八年（公元一五五九年）威尼斯著名作家拉馬司·沃阿著的《中國茶》和《中國旅行記》兩書。葡萄牙傳天主教的第一人，一五六〇年將中國茶葉傳播天主教的宣傳，引飲茶之風波及到英、法等國。只要投錢，隨時都可以取飲。據唐人封演《封氏聞見記》記載：開元（公元七二三至七四一年）中從山東、河北的部份地區，直至當時的首都長安，「城市多開店舖，煎茶賣之，不問道俗，投錢取飲，其茶自江淮而來，舟車相繼，所在山積，色額甚多」同書又說：「…古人亦飲茶耳，但不如今人溺之甚，窮日盡夜，殆成風俗，起自中地，流於塞外。」可知唐時飲茶之風，已由南方傳播到黃河北岸，並且遠播到塞外西北各地。不但如此，這時已由南方傳播到飲茶的奇葩，也很快染上飲茶嗜好。茶逐漸成為他們日常生活中不可缺少的必需品。

荷蘭人和英國人都視為「貢品」和奢侈品。隨着茶葉輸入量的不斷增加，價格逐漸下降，成為家庭日常的飲料。後來，英國人成為世界上最大的茶客，英國成為飲茶費量最多的國家。到雍正年間，美國飲茶之風也由荷蘭人傳到歐洲去了。茶也很快從歐洲和亞洲甚至世界各地的鄉村。早在五世紀的時候，它的種類和飲茶方法等知識傳入歐洲。明朝萬曆年間，荷蘭人從我國購運大量茶葉，除供給國內消費外，還轉運到美洲殖民地。一六四四年，英人在廈門設立商務機構，專門販茶，以廈門人稱茶的發音為「te」而把茶的英文名拼為「tea」。以後瑞典、丹麥、法國、西班牙、德國、匈牙利等國的商船也紛紛慕名而至，都從中國販運茶葉。一六六二年，嗜好飲茶的葡萄牙公主凱瑟琳嫁給英皇查理二世以後，英國第一個飲茶的皇后，從此飲茶風靡全英國。朝廷中風行的葡萄酒、燒酒等烈性飲料，隨着茶最初傳到歐洲時價格高昂，被視為「貢品」和飲料。

這期間，西後東來，並在本國上層社會流傳飲茶。在歐洲各國的茶葉，最初提到我國茶葉的是明世宗嘉靖三十八年（公元一五五九年）威尼斯著名作家拉馬司·沃阿著的《中國茶》和《中國旅行記》兩書。葡萄牙傳天主教的第一人，一五六〇年將中國茶葉品類及飲茶方法傳入歐洲。明代神宗萬曆三十五年（公元一六〇七年）荷蘭海船自爪哇來澳門販茶轉運歐洲，這是茶葉直接銷往歐洲的最早記錄。以後，茶葉就成為荷蘭販運往遠東的最重要的飲料。到了清初順治、康熙年間，英商人從我國購運大量茶葉。

鐵觀音奇種（歐洲各國的商人……這地區開運中國茶葉，並在本國上層社會流傳飲茶。在歐洲的文獻中……）

六安包種

地區發現和開始利用茶葉以後，經過一千多年的漫長時間，至西漢時代，飲茶傳播地區逐漸廣闊。在春秋戰國後期及西漢初年，曾發生過幾次大規模的戰爭，造成了人口的大遷徙。特別是秦統一中國以後，促進了經濟和文化的交流，四川、雲南一帶的茶樹栽培、茶葉加工及飲用方法，開始向當時的經濟、政治、文化中心陝西、河南等地傳播，這是陝西、河南成為北方古老茶區的原因。

王褒是西漢時期四川資中的一位儒生，到成都作客，寄居在他亡友的妻子楊惠家裡。此可說，兩晉、南北朝……茶的起源距今當有三四千年了。據《僮約》記載，王褒喜愛飲酒，時常到寡婦楊氏的家僮便了去打酒，不久楊氏將便了賣給王褒，成為王褒專用的家僮，便了不滿。王褒是我國最早和最有價值的茶葉……「武陽買茶」、「烹茶盡具」兩句。武陽，即今四川彭山縣東，距彭山縣境十市里，為漢代主要的產茶區之一，附近山縣約十市里，為漢代……「僅約」中涉及茶的有兩處，所立契約就是王褒和茶的一種契約，約）是一種比較珍貴的飲料。

此契約訂立於神爵三年（公元前五十九年）正月十五日，訂定了每天從事茶事勞役，成都買茶，其中涉及茶的有「烹茶盡具」、「武陽買茶」兩句。

《僮約》（奇戲之意），寄居在他亡友的妻子楊惠家裡，便了
「策問」王褒是西漢時期四川
獻。「武陽買茶」、「烹茶盡具」。

战国后期以及社会发生了几次大规模的战争，造成了人口的大迁徙。特别是秦统一中国以后，促进了经济和文化的交流，四川、云南一带的茶树栽培、茶叶加工及饮用方法，开始向当时的经济、政治、文化中心陕西、河南等地传播，这是陕西、河南成为北方古老茶区的原因。同时，传播

到肚子里，就从下到上，从上到下，到处流动洗涤，好似把肠胃洗涤得干干净净。他就称这种绿叶为「查」。以后人们叫成「茶」了。神农成年累月地爬山涉水，全靠茶来解救。茶和其他植物一样，从发现到利用，需要经过一段漫长的岁月。当原始人类发现茶叶对人体的医疗效用以后，对茶就开始注意和重视起来。据古籍记载，茶叶最初只作药用。到了春秋时代，已经提到用茶叶作菜饮，但没有定论。有许多文献的记载，

种开着乳白色花朵的树上的嫩叶，发现这种绿叶真奇怪，一片片

始于春秋战国时代，有的人认为的「秦人取蜀（四川）」而后始有茗饮之事」。即产茶和饮茶始于秦汉时以后，记载着茶事如西汉扬雄《蜀都赋》中就有读美茶的句子：「百芬芳」，蔓茶茨都、翠紫青黄」。在《赵飞燕别传》中，有一段关于汉代饮茶的记述，汉成帝崩，「后（即帝后）寝惊啼甚久，侍者呼问，方觉，乃言：「适吾梦中见帝，帝自云中赐吾坐，帝命进茶。左右奏帝，后向日待帝不谨，不合啜此茶。」反映出在西汉时期，茶已成为皇室中的一种饮料了。又据史料记载「汉王

作者说饮茶

家说纷纭，

我国饮茶究竟

曾在江苏宜兴茗岭「课童艺茶」：汉代江临海盖竹山有仙翁茶园，浙江名士往年回纥入

殆成风俗，所在山积，色额甚多」同书又说：「...古人亦饮茶耳，但不如今人溺之甚，穷日尽夜，

据《僮约》的

水品饮等作了精湛的论述。在唐代，南北城镇已出现了茶肆。日相仿佛的茶肆了。

六安包种

山东、河北的部分地区，直至当时的首都长安「城市多开店铺，煎茶卖之，不问道俗，投钱取饮。」

唐朝李肇著的《国史补》记载：唐朝

福寿宫茶莊

状元梅花水片

福茗堂
本號在太子行
開張檢提細嫩
茶葉加芽揉造
發行
香港中環遮打道太子行
商場二百二十一室

金
貢品烏龍

鐵觀音

普洱

六